START
FRESH

P9-BZY-155

START FRESH

START FRESH

Your Child's Jump Start to
Lifelong Healthy Eating

TYLER FLORENCE

Photographs by John Lee

This book is intended as a reference volume only, not as a medical manual. The information given here is designed to help you make informed decisions about your child's health. It is not intended as a substitute for any treatment that may have been prescribed for your child by your doctor. If you suspect that your child has a medical problem, we urge you to seek competent medical help.

Mention of specific companies, organizations, or authorities in this book does not imply endorsement by the author or publisher, nor does mention of specific companies, organizations, or authorities imply that they endorse this book, its author, or the publisher.

Internet addresses and telephone numbers given in this book were accurate at the time it went to press.

© 2011 by Tyler Florence
Photographs © 2011 by John Lee

All rights reserved. No part of this publication may be reproduced or transmitted in any form or by any means, electronic or mechanical, including photocopying, recording, or any other information storage and retrieval system, without the written permission of the publisher.

Rodale books may be purchased for business or promotional use or for special sales. For information, please write to:

Special Markets Department, Rodale, Inc., 733 Third Avenue, New York, NY 10017

Printed in the United States of America
Rodale Inc. makes every effort to use acid-free ♾, recycled paper ♻.

Design and illustrations by Kara Plikaitis

SPROUT ® is a registered trademark of Sprout Foods, Inc.

Library of Congress Cataloging-in-Publication Data
    Start fresh : your child's jump start to lifelong healthy eating / Tyler Florence ; photographs by John Lee.
        p.   cm.
    Includes index.
    ISBN 978-1-60961-194-1 hardcover
    1. Cooking.   2. Infants—Nutrition.   3. Infants—Health and hygiene.   I. Title.
    TX714.F6356 2011
    641.5′6222—dc22
                            2011011484

Distributed to the trade by Macmillan
2 4 6 8 10 9 7 5 3 1 hardcover

🌱 RODALE

We inspire and enable people to improve their
lives and the world around them.
www.rodalebooks.com

THIS BOOK IS DEDICATED TO MY FAMILY:

My children,
Miles, Hayden, and Dorothy;

my wife, Tolan;

and my two best friends,
Jake Bacon and
the new baby, Frank Jr.

CONTENTS

Foreword

One balmy California evening not long ago, Tyler Florence and I savored a scrumptious dinner together with our families and friends. I had recently finished writing *Feeding Baby Green,* a safe, simple program for helping kids develop the ability to recognize and enjoy healthy amounts of good food (what we call Nutritional Intelligence), and our conversation naturally moved to the way we as a nation are feeding ourselves and especially our children. Sadly, we all agreed there was tremendous room for improvement, as evidenced by rising rates of obesity and a general unwillingness to try new things among many of the children we meet each day.

As a pediatrician I have come to understand that great food is central to great health and that sharing meals is pivotal to strengthening our connections as family. So you can imagine my excitement as Tyler shared the sights, sounds, textures, and tastes of his culinary vision—a celebration of *real* food that families could enjoy together. The conversation around that table was electric as ideas sparked to and fro.

For too long parents have been hampered by a sense of fear when it comes to feeding their babies. Fear of allergies, fear of not being able to provide safe, nutritious meals without a baby-food jar, and fear that, even if they could, it would be unpleasant, hard work.

In 2008, the American Academy of Pediatrics reassured us that there is no convincing evidence that delaying even items such as fish, eggs, and foods containing peanuts beyond 4 to 6 months lessens the incidence of allergies in children. In 2011, Tyler Florence assures us that cooking for our young children can be beautiful, delicious, and fun.

We're living in an exciting time when it comes to feeding our youngest children. Over the last two decades we've learned a lot about how taste preferences develop during the first few years of life, starting even before birth. For instance, we now know that children tend to form lasting preferences for the sources of food, the styles of food, the colors of food, and the tastes of food that they eat and enjoy on a regular basis as they move from stage to stage during those early years.

This early window of opportunity gradually closes as something called *neophobia*—a physical distrust of unfamiliar foods that often lingers through the grade-school years—tends to set in. Dealing with neophobia is its own adventure, but you can make that transition a lot more rewarding for you both by celebrating a broad variety of foods and flavors during your child's more receptive, exploratory years.

You're holding such a celebration in your hands. As you thumb through the pages and delight in the mouthwatering photographs—and later, as you stand in the kitchen and sample the recipes you've made—you'll find Tyler's love of great food contagious. So will your children.

Bon appétit!

ALAN GREENE, MD, FAAP
Attending Pediatrician, Packard Children's Hospital at Stanford University
Author of *Feeding Baby Green*
"Let every child's first grain be a whole grain. They won't mind, they'll thank us for it."

START FRESH

from the
VERY START

Introduction

As a chef and father of three, cooking for my children means more than just going through the motions of getting dinner on the table. It's about forging the foundation for a healthy relationship with food that will last for the rest of their lives.

Because my wife and I cook with our children daily, they get a chance to taste everything. Ever since they were old enough to sit up, we've made sure they had a front row seat, banging on pots and pans on the floor of our kitchen while we sliced and stirred and sautéed. I always give them a spoonful of whatever I'm working on, so they are constantly being exposed to new tastes and textures. Of course they don't love everything, but that's not the point. My objective is to open their minds to the world of real, whole foods and to expose them to a variety of different fresh ingredients and flavors from the very beginning. In other words, to start fresh from the very start.

As parents, we are bombarded by marketing intent on convincing us that we don't know how to feed our children. Food producers would have us believe that the Big 5 (pizza, hot dogs, chicken nuggets, french fries, and burgers) are the only things kids will eat, that chicken nuggets pressed into the shape of a dinosaur are a healthy part of a meal. It's insulting. More importantly, once children get hooked on the taste of processed fat and salt, it's a long haul to get them back.

Children begin to make conscious decisions about what they like and don't like from the moment they are born. Infants have a heightened ability to detect sweet, bitter, and sour—in fact their sense of taste is 10 times as keen as an adult's. So the moment children move away from breast milk or formula—usually at around 4 to 6 months—is the time you can make a gigantic difference in what they consider delicious, the way they eat, and the nutrients they put into their bodies. And all you have to do is cook for them.

Most commercial baby foods put very little thought into the taste of their final product, and their advertising even makes references to "winning the battle" or "test of wills" when it comes to feeding children. Even though they can't speak yet, your children are trying to tell you something: They don't like what you are feeding them.

Luckily, nature gave small children the defense system of a gag reflex, and trying to get a child to eat something she simply doesn't like won't be solved by all the choo-choo train or airplane tricks in the world. Hey, we've all been there!

Baby food has baggage. Until recently the industry hadn't really changed much since prepared baby food was first introduced in the 1950s. While jarred baby food offered parents convenience, too often it came in the form of mushy, green mash that tasted more like the cardboard box the jars came in than the wholesome vegetables they were trying to impersonate. When we launched our organic baby food company, Sprout, in 2008, my partner Max Mackenzie, his wife, Jillian, and I set up a booth at the Healthy Baby & Child Expo in San Antonio, Texas, and offered samples of eight of our baby foods. The convention center was packed with people and other companies in the industry. Parents walked up to the booth and asked what we were serving. When we invited them to taste our "delicious organic baby food," they immediately shook their heads and said "no thanks," but handed the cup of carrot, mango, and apple puree to their small children. We were shocked to realize that most of the parents expected baby food to taste terrible (well, I'm actually not shocked at all—in the case of many commercial baby foods, they're right) and that they didn't think their kids would know the difference. After a little coaxing, and seeing their babies licking the spoons clean, a few brave souls actually tasted it and all said, "Wow, I had no idea baby food could taste this good." (We also saw a few executives from one of the old-guard baby food companies try a few samples and walk away hastily banging on their PDAs. Now that's an e-mail I would love to have read.)

As parents of this new generation, we have a leg up on what our parents knew about health, nutrition, and obesity. It's time to stop making excuses about what we put on our tables and in our children's bodies and recognize that companies that produce cheap food are not doing you any favors. With information so readily available, we can take control of our children's health and well-being. It's time to turn over a new leaf and get away from food that is nutritionally bankrupt. Embrace the colors and flavors and wholesome qualities of fresh food. You owe it to your children. With the recipes in this book, you and I can do it together.

IT'S TIME TO **START FRESH**

The Basics

GETTING STARTED

WHAT YOU'LL NEED

Making baby food is easy, so we're not talking about accumulating a lot of unnecessary kitchen equipment. As a matter of fact, you probably already have everything you'll need on hand. Most of the recipes in this book use one of two cooking methods: steaming or roasting. Both are very straightforward techniques that can be accomplished with just a few essential pieces of equipment.

FOR STEAMING

You'll need a large pot with a tight-fitting lid. If you find a pot that comes with its own steamer basket that fits inside, fantastic; if not, you can manage just fine without it—a pasta colander that can sit over the pot or a collapsible steamer insert that fits inside works just as well. A Chinese bamboo steamer with a tight-fitting lid is also amazing for steaming tender vegetables. They are really cheap and they last a really long time. I've had mine for years. So take your pick. And that's it. Pretty simple, right?

FOR ROASTING

Roasting is even easier than steaming. All you'll need are a few baking sheets and your oven. Don't cook on flimsy cookie sheets; go for sturdy rimmed baking sheets. You can pick them up at most kitchen stores or, if you want to go on a field trip, check out a local restaurant supply store. (Look it up online; every town has one.) They will have rimmed baking sheets, which are called sheet pans. Ask for a half-sheet pan, which measures 18 x 13 inches; most home ovens cannot accommodate a full-sheet pan, which is 18 x 26 inches. They will also have everything that makes a restaurant tick. I can spend hours in a restaurant supply shop.

FOR PUREEING

To make supersmooth purees for very young babies starting on solid food for the first time, I prefer a blender to a food processor because it produces a much smoother puree. (If you want to splurge, a high-speed blender does the job best and most quickly of all.) While a food processor can chop foods finely, it doesn't truly puree the way a blender does. Once your baby is ready for purees with a little texture, around when they start getting teeth, you can switch to a food processor and pulse or grind the food to the texture you and your baby prefer, from coarse to fine.

STORING AND REHEATING BABY FOOD SAFELY

Most of the recipes in this book make 6 to 8 child-size servings, which allows you to put several portions in the bank for future meals each time you cook for your baby. Fortunately most purees reheat very well as long as they are stored properly. So how do you keep and reheat food safely? The best way to store baby food in the fridge or freezer is in BPA-free plastic storage containers. Place pureed or fork-mashed foods in a storage container just large enough to hold it and cover tightly; the food can then be refrigerated for one or two days. If you haven't used all the leftovers within about 48 hours, you can freeze anything that remains. Spoon the puree into ice cube trays and freeze until solid, then transfer to freezer-weight plastic bags to store and defrost as needed. (Each cube is equal to about 2 tablespoons.) Be sure to press as much air out of the bag as possible and label the bag with the date and contents. Frozen foods should be used within one month.

To reheat, allow frozen food to defrost overnight in the refrigerator or transfer directly from the freezer to the microwave; never defrost at room temperature, as this can allow harmful bacteria to develop. No plastic containers of any kind should be used when reheating baby food in the microwave; transfer the food to a container made of lead-free porcelain, a glass bowl, or lead-free table china.

Reheat at 50 percent power in 60-second increments, stirring each time to eliminate any hot spots. You can also reheat it in a saucepan over low heat, stirring often to prevent scorching or sticking. In either case, reheat just until warm, not hot, and always test for temperature before offering to your baby.

A note on BPA and something to think about . . .

In the last year or two, a lot of very valuable information about storing food and water in plastics and, most importantly, reheating in plastics has come to light.

Bisphenol A (also called BPA) and phthalates are chemical softeners that make hard plastic soft and moldable. These softening agents are found in everything from plastic wrap and plastic food storage bags to plastic food containers, baby bottles, children's toys, and sippy cups.

Bisphenol A has been used in industrial plastic production since the 1930s and is known as an environmental estrogen, which, once ingested, acts as a hormone disrupter. It has been linked to breast cancer, fetal brain developmental issues, obesity, disruption of thyroid function, early puberty (in girls), and increased risk of cancer. In short, nothing you want anywhere near your child's food.

In 2008, a team of scientists from the University of Cincinnati found that when both new and used polycarbonate sport bottles were exposed to boiling water, BPA was released into the water inside the bottle at a level 55 times higher than when the same plastic bottles were exposed to room-temperature water. These findings sent justifiable waves of concern throughout the world, with Canada and the European Union quickly banning the use of BPA in baby bottle production. In 2010, Canada banned all BPA plastic production and classified the chemical as toxic.

Although the United States has not yet taken sweeping steps to ban the chemical, in March of 2009, bills were introduced in both houses of Congress to ban the use of BPA in all food and beverage containers.

Introduced in the House by Rep. Edward Markey of Massachusetts and in the Senate by Sen. Dianne Feinstein of California, the proposed legislation would ban the sale of any reusable consumer beverage products and containers like baby bottles and sippy cups that contain BPA and prohibit other food and beverage containers, including those for canned foods and formula, that contain the chemical from entering the market.

On BPA plastics, Senator Feinstein writes:

I have been working hard to get BPA out of our food products, but have been blocked by chemical company lobbyists. We have made some progress with some major manufacturers and retailers who have begun to phase out their BPA products.

I'm not going to give up and am currently working to pass legislation that will get this chemical out of our children's products. Moms, dads, grandparents, and other consumers and voters all over the country have written to me asking for BPA to be removed from their products. We should not use our kids as guinea pigs with a chemical that can seriously harm their immediate and long-term health. I encourage everyone to write to their members of Congress about this issue and continue to look for those companies that are already using BPA alternatives.

At the time of writing *Start Fresh* in January of 2011, the BPA-Free Kids Act has been reintroduced into Congress by Representative Markey and Senator Feinstein. Let's hope this time it sticks. In the meantime, legislation has been introduced in 30 states across the country to ban BPA plastics locally. Lawmakers are getting pressure from constituents coast to coast to get this chemical out of the marketplace.

But without the protection of US federal laws banning chemicals like BPA, and with international trade bringing products in from all over the world (including areas where environmental laws are lax), we are on our own. You have to read labels carefully. If a plastic food storage container or sippy cup doesn't say BPA-free, it's not. And it's not worth exposing your child to the possible risks.

In the meantime, to reduce the risk of liability, most major baby bottle manufacturers in the United States have implemented self-imposed withdrawals of children's products containing BPA—a solid step in the right direction.

- Honey
- All cow's milk, pasteurized, unpasteurized, or raw
- Unpasteurized juices, such as fresh apple cider
- Soft rind, unpasteurized cheeses
- Raw eggs (both yolks and whites)
- Raw sprouts
- Raw or very rare meats
- Raw fish
- Raw or cooked shellfish (cooked shellfish is OK after 6 months)
- Luncheon meats

A FEW QUICK FEEDING RULES

What you *don't* feed your newborn is just as important as what you *do* feed him. Most pediatricians agree there are a number of seemingly wholesome foods that should be avoided until a child has reached 12 months, as these foods may contain bacteria or spores that his digestive tract is not yet equipped to handle and could result in some pretty nasty stuff. After the age of 12 months pediatricians generally consider all foods safe, as a child's immune system has developed enough to protect him from harmful bacteria by this stage.

I've been consulting with Dr. Alan Greene, author of many great books for parents, about when it's appropriate to start children on certain foods, and I strongly recommend that you use this book as a guide in conjunction with your own pediatrician or family doctor, too. That said, few pediatricians still subscribe to the rule of "One new food per week." Food allergies, though present in only 6 percent of children, do occur. However, it is becoming increasingly clear that early introduction of new foods is actually *less* likely to cause allergic reactions than waiting until your child is older, and sampling many new foods will help her learn to appreciate a broader range of flavors.

After that, it all comes down to taste trials, and this part is a lot of fun— and maybe a little messy. Most pediatricians consider 4 to 6 months the perfect time to start introducing solid food into your child's diet. (Formula-fed babies may be ready as early as 4 months while breast-fed babies, who are getting more complete nutrition, may be happy with breast milk alone even beyond 6 months.) This is when she's starting to mimic your moves, and thinks peek-a-boo is the greatest game ever invented. She can hold her head up by herself, can sit in a high chair, is able to close her mouth around a spoon, and can move food from the front of her mouth to the back. Also you'll start to notice that formula or breast milk alone doesn't really cut it anymore, as children put on weight rapidly at this stage and constantly need to be satiated. When it's time to move to solid food, it's time.

Breast milk, formula, and iron-rich cereals such as rice, barley, and oats should be an important part of their diet during this period, as weight gain helps in the development of the child's immune system. At this point you should just consider solid food a supplemental form of nutrients (after all, "An apple a day keeps the doctor away" is not just an old adage). Remember, eating solids will be very new territory. Babies naturally curl their tongues in a suckle motion as they try to suck from a spoon; getting your child to lay his tongue flat as he eats from a spoon will be the first point of business. After a week, he'll get the hang of it and his tongue will start to adapt to this new way of taking in sustenance, allowing him to get more food into his mouth and stomach.

ONE STEP AT A TIME

While there is no limit on how many new foods you can introduce to your baby in a given week or day, offering simple single-ingredient purees at first makes it easier to keep track of what he does or doesn't like.

Don't give up if his first reaction to a new flavor is not entirely enthusiastic. You may have to offer certain foods a few times, with varying degrees of success, to get a sense of which foods can go on the menu permanently—and which are simply nonstarters. Babies have a hyperacute sense of taste, which functions as a defense mechanism against ingesting potentially harmful foods. They naturally reject bitter flavors, because in nature most things that are poisonous are bitter. (Funny how that works.) Sweet is their favorite flavor, as it suggests the pleasing taste of breast milk, the food most likely to ensure their survival. (Again, funny how that works.) I say start with carrots—they're sweet, but deeply nutritious. And always go with organic if possible.

Tracking Your Child's Success

When starting on solid food, you'll want a way to track your child's progress. You can photocopy the worksheet on the next page, but a wall calendar or datebook, for you tiger moms out there, will do just fine, too. Just choose something you can take notes on. These notes are very important to share with your pediatrician as you both track the successes and the few inevitable failures of any new foods that are introduced.

NEW FOODS: WEEK __ __ / __

MON	TUES	WED	THURS	FRI	SAT	SUN

Comments: _____

_____

NEW FOODS: WEEK __ __ / __

MON	TUES	WED	THURS	FRI	SAT	SUN

Comments: _____

_____

NEW FOODS: WEEK __ __ / __

MON	TUES	WED	THURS	FRI	SAT	SUN

Comments: _____

_____

NEW FOODS: WEEK __ __ / __

MON	TUES	WED	THURS	FRI	SAT	SUN

Comments: _____

_____

NEW FOODS: WEEK __ __ / __

MON	TUES	WED	THURS	FRI	SAT	SUN

Comments: _____

_____

NEW FOODS: WEEK __ __ / __

MON	TUES	WED	THURS	FRI	SAT	SUN

Comments: _____

_____

NEW FOODS: WEEK __ __ / __

MON	TUES	WED	THURS	FRI	SAT	SUN

Comments: _____

_____

NEW FOODS: WEEK __ __ / __

MON	TUES	WED	THURS	FRI	SAT	SUN

Comments: _____

_____

A note on ORGANICS
and something to think about . . .

I don't think there is a parent out there who would knowingly give her children chemicals, but it is a fact that 98 percent of all sprayed pesticides reach a target other than the intended one. So guess where those pesticides go? Into the water, soil, and air that we breathe. It's what's known as pesticide drift. But the health impact is even worse than the environmental impact. The American Medical Association recommends little to no exposure to pesticides and strongly recommends safer practices. The World Health Organization (WHO) and the United Nations' environmental

program have determined that at least 3 million farm workers in developing countries become gravely ill due to pesticide exposure, and 18,000 of those die each year from pesticide poisoning. Pesticides, herbicides, and insecticides have been linked to everything from lymphoma and leukemia to birth defects and neuro-developmental issues. So the question is, if your food is not Certified Organic, can you trust that it is free of unwanted chemicals? I can't trust food that's not Certified Organic and I don't think there is much debate anymore about the value of chemical-free organic foods to your health or to the health of your children.

A Question of Price

It's true that most organic produce is slightly more expensive than chemically grown produce. As the marketplace shifts with growing consumer demand for organic produce (which is growing at a rate of 21 percent per year in the United States), that price differential should be leveled very quickly. It's simple supply and demand. If the demand for organic produce continues to rise, boutique farming will become more efficient, more "mainstream" to meet consumer demand, and the supply will increase, thus bringing down the overall cost of organics through competitive pricing. The more you make and sell, the cheaper it gets—it's Economics 101. (Just think about

the price of flat-screen televisions a decade ago versus today.) You have a lot of pull with your wallet. If you demand better, more transparent food handling practices and are willing to put your money where your mouth is, your local grocery store will hear you and prices *will* come down. A decade from now, hopefully large-scale farming will catch up with the modern organics movement and price will no longer be an issue.

SINGLE-INGREDIENT PUREES

Steamed Carrot Puree

FIRST FOODS

Now is your chance to make a gigantic difference in your children's lives. If you don't want them running into the arms of the fast-food clown the first time they taste a french fry, you have to expose them to the freshest flavors and the most densely nutritious food you possibly can. French fries taste good, but fresh vegetables taste better. Not everything will work, but that's OK. It will all start to stack up with every new taste and every neural connection. Remember, your goal is to create a lifelong vegetable fan. This is the fun part.

As soon as your child has gotten the hang of eating from a spoon with rice or other cereals, she is ready to move on to single-ingredient purees. At this stage we're looking for a supersmooth puree with no pulp or chunks whatsoever, so use a blender, not a food processor, to make your purees. Small babies have a gag reflex that's triggered by even small particles, so the smoother the puree, the more likely you are to have success, the greater the trust factor you will develop, and the more they will enjoy mealtime. Carrots, butternut squash, and apples are really good places to start.

STEAMING VERSUS BOILING

When you boil vegetables, you extract valuable nutrients that are poured down the drain when the cooking water is discarded. When you cook them *over* boiling water, either in a steamer basket, bamboo steamer, or strainer of some kind, you lose next to nothing. The steaming process leaves every bite tender, moist, and densely concentrated with vitamins. Beyond that, I've often found that boiled vegetables, especially if they've been overcooked, can develop a bitter flavor that children can pick up on right away. In my experience, they just spit this kind of food out. So let's save the vitamins, flavor, and some laundry. Steaming is better.

STEAMED CARROT PUREE

Now let's cook something. This recipe is more about technique than specific quantities or ratios, so we can just talk it through.

Cut the greens off of 1 bunch of organic carrots. If the carrots are small, there is no need to peel them; just give them a good scrubbing. The skin of larger carrots can taste bitter, so it's a good idea to peel them. Slice the carrots evenly into circles and set aside.

Pour about 1 cup of distilled or filtered water into a large pot and bring to a boil over high heat. Place the carrot slices in a steamer basket or colander and carefully place over the boiling water. Cover with the lid and steam until the carrots are tender. This usually takes about 10 minutes, depending on how big the carrots are and how thickly you slice them.

The carrots puree better when they're hot, so transfer to a clean blender (that means wash the margarita smell out before you use it to make your baby purees). Start on low and let the teeth of the blender grab the carrots and get a little motion going in the bottom. Add a few tablespoons of the hot water you used to steam the veggies if needed to smooth out the texture, but no salt, no fat (i.e., butter or oil) at this stage. That will come later, when your baby is a few months older.

Now, taste the carrot puree and notice how delicious the clean flavor of freshly steamed carrots is. No, really, spend a minute with the flavor in your mouth and really taste it. You taste bright carotene, subtle pine notes, earthy sugars. It's quite a complex flavor if you close your eyes and study it.

Next, taste your carrots side by side with pureed carrot baby food from a jar. There's really no contest; it's shocking how much better homemade steamed carrots can be than the stuff in the jar.

Now comes the best part, watching your baby's eyes light up when he tastes it. Just watching him roll a vegetable puree around in his mouth and study the flavor is fascinating. This is where you can play choo-choo train all day.

One thing to remember: Temperature is a big deal for babies. They like food best when it is at warm body temperature. Feel a small amount with the back of your finger. If you can't really detect the temperature, meaning it's not too hot, not too cold, you're good to go. Think Goldilocks's porridge.

And that's it, that's all there is to making the move to real food. The same technique is perfect for just about everything from green beans to zucchini, butternut squash, spinach, sweet corn, cauliflower—you name it.

Introduce as many of these simple purees as you like for 2 months or so. After that, you are ready to go to the next level.

SWEET POTATO PUREE

MAKES FOUR ½-CUP SERVINGS
OR TWO 1-CUP SERVINGS

1 pound (2 medium) sweet potatoes, peeled and cut into 1-inch chunks

Bring 3 cups of water to a boil in a pot with a steamer insert or use a collapsible basket. Reduce the heat to a brisk simmer, add the potatoes, and steam for 12 to 15 minutes, or until tender when pierced with a fork.

Transfer the potato chunks to a blender and puree until very smooth, adding some of the steaming liquid to thin the consistency if needed.

SUMMER SQUASH OR ZUCCHINI PUREE

MAKES FOUR ½-CUP SERVINGS
OR TWO 1-CUP SERVINGS

1 pound (3 medium) summer squash or zucchini, unpeeled and cut into 1-inch chunks

Bring 3 cups of water to a boil in a pot with a steamer insert or use a collapsible basket. Reduce the heat to a brisk simmer, add the squash, and steam for 8 to 10 minutes, or until tender when pierced with a fork.

Transfer the squash pieces to a blender and puree until very smooth, adding some of the steaming liquid to thin the consistency if needed.

ASPARAGUS PUREE

MAKES FOUR ½-CUP SERVINGS
OR TWO 1-CUP SERVINGS

1 pound (10 medium stalks) asparagus, washed and tough stems removed

Bring 3 cups of water to a boil in a pot with a steamer insert or use a collapsible basket. Reduce the heat to a brisk simmer, add the asparagus, and steam for 8 to 10 minutes, or until tender when pierced with a fork.

Transfer the asparagus to a blender and puree until very smooth, adding some of the steaming liquid to thin the consistency if needed.

BROCCOLI PUREE

MAKES FOUR ½-CUP SERVINGS
OR TWO 1-CUP SERVINGS

1 pound broccoli, florets and stems cut into 1-inch pieces

Bring 3 cups of water to a boil in a pot with a steamer insert or use a collapsible basket. Reduce the heat to a brisk simmer, add the broccoli, and steam for 8 to 10 minutes, or until tender when pierced with a fork.

Transfer the broccoli to a blender and puree until very smooth, adding some of the steaming liquid to thin the consistency if needed.

PEAR
PUREE

MAKES FOUR ½-CUP SERVINGS
OR TWO 1-CUP SERVINGS

1 pound (2 medium) firm pears,
stemmed, cored, and cut into
1-inch chunks

Bring 3 cups of water to a boil in a pot with a steamer insert or use a collapsible basket. Reduce the heat to a brisk simmer, add the pears, and steam for 12 to 15 minutes, or until tender when pierced with a fork.

Transfer the pear chunks to a blender and puree until very smooth, adding some of the steaming liquid to thin the consistency if needed.

SPINACH
PUREE

MAKES TWO ½-CUP SERVINGS
OR ONE 1-CUP SERVINGS

1 pound fresh spinach, rinsed very
well and tough stems removed

Bring 3 cups of water to a boil in a pot with a steamer insert or use a collapsible basket. Reduce the heat to a brisk simmer, add the spinach, and steam for 12 to 15 minutes, or until tender.

Transfer the spinach to a blender and puree until very smooth, adding some of the steaming liquid to thin the consistency if needed

TURNIP OR
RUTABAGA PUREE

MAKES FOUR ½-CUP SERVINGS
OR TWO 1-CUP SERVINGS

1 pound (3 or 4 medium)
turnips or rutabagas,
washed well, trimmed,
and cut into 1-inch chunks

Bring 3 cups of water to a boil in a pot with a steamer insert or use a collapsible basket. Reduce the heat to a brisk simmer, add the turnips, and steam for 12 to 15 minutes, or until tender when pierced with a fork.

Transfer the turnip chunks to a blender and puree until very smooth, adding some of the steaming liquid to thin the consistency if needed.

CAULIFLOWER
PUREE

MAKES FOUR ½-CUP SERVINGS
OR TWO 1-CUP SERVINGS

1 pound (1 small head)
cauliflower florets

Bring 3 cups of water to a boil in a pot with a steamer insert or use a collapsible basket. Reduce the heat to a brisk simmer, add the cauliflower, and steam for 12 to 15 minutes, or until tender when pierced with a fork.

Transfer the cauliflower to a blender and puree until very smooth, adding some of the steaming liquid to thin the consistency if needed.

POTATO PUREE

MAKES FOUR ½-CUP SERVINGS
OR TWO 1-CUP SERVINGS

1 pound (1 large or 2 small) Idaho or russet potatoes, washed well and cut into 1-inch chunks

Bring 3 cups of water to a boil in a pot with a steamer insert or use a collapsible basket. Reduce the heat to a brisk simmer, add the potatoes, and steam for 14 to 16 minutes, or until tender when pierced with a fork.

Transfer the potato chunks to a blender and puree until very smooth, adding some of the steaming liquid to thin the consistency if needed.

PARSNIP PUREE

MAKES FOUR ½-CUP SERVINGS
OR TWO 1-CUP SERVINGS

1 pound medium parsnips, peeled and cut into 1-inch chunks

Bring 3 cups of water to a boil in a pot with a steamer insert or use a collapsible basket. Reduce the heat to a brisk simmer, add the parsnips, and steam for 15 to 17 minutes, or until tender when pierced with a fork.

Transfer the parsnips to a blender and puree until very smooth, adding some of the steaming liquid to thin the consistency if needed.

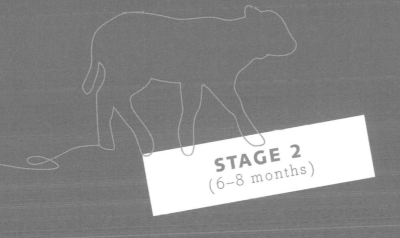

STAGE 2
(6–8 months)

FLAVOR
COMBOS

Roasted Broccoli with
Parmesan and Olive Oil

Once your little one has been eating solid food for a few months, it's time to step it up with more complex meals. You can either offer a pairing of single-ingredient purees at each meal or create flavor combinations by pureeing different ingredients together. At this point your child is ready to progress from simple, clean flavors to multi-ingredient dishes that are savory, well-seasoned nutrient bombs.

Many of the recipes I developed for my baby food company, Sprout, are based on the flavor combinations and basic sauce techniques that I've used in restaurants for years, so don't think of these purees simply as baby food; once you've tried the next handful of recipes you'll have a whole new repertoire of fruit and vegetable sauces to go with roasted meats and fish and interesting purees that can round out an otherwise straightforward meal.

Once you start to try these more sophisticated purees, I'm betting you will be blown away by the flavors, and so will your child. Developing your child's sense of taste at this age is just as important as developing social, cognitive, and motor skills. The older children get, the harder it is to supervise everything they put in their mouths. By broadening your child's palate early, you'll get a leg up on the food scientists who are busy developing unhealthy processed foods aimed at rocking your child's taste buds with artificial flavors, fat, salt, and cheap ingredients. Use the recipes in this section to expand your child's culinary horizons. They are supereasy and everything stores really well, so you can cook for several days in one afternoon. And by all means, feel free to use the techniques as a guide to create your own flavor combinations that will blow your child away.

ROASTING

By now your little guy should be open to a variety of foods, and if he is sprouting a few teeth, he's ready for a little texture. The process of roasting meat or vegetables at moderately high heat is really your best tool for winning your children over to what they may still consider the dark side of eating: fresh vegetables. The roasting process brings out food's natural sugars and deeply develops its flavor in a way that boiling and even steaming simply can't. And I'm telling you, it makes everything taste incredible. There is not one vegetable that my children will refuse to eat if it's been roasted. It's my number one cooking tip for parents who are struggling to get their children to eat more vegetables.

Once the food is cooked you can puree it until smooth, chop it to a fine mash, or simply fork-mash it to make a puree with a little texture for new teeth. The whole process is supersimple and all you need to get started is a rimmed baking sheet or roasting pan, a little olive oil, and an oven.

The science behind roasting and why it is a superior cooking technique for your child's next steps in baby food is fairly simple. Roasting at moderate heat, say around 350°F, turns natural starches into sugars and evaporates useless water. When the water evaporates, the flavor becomes more concentrated. Then the sugars caramelize, creating a supersavory taste that is perfectly balanced with natural sweetness. Add a touch of salt and a little drizzle of olive oil over roasted green beans, Brussels sprouts, summer squash, broccoli—you name it, it all works. Don't be afraid to use olive oil. It not only aids in the caramelization and tastes great, but its "good fats" also act as a delivery system, helping the body absorb the vitamins and nutrients in food. It's good *and* good for you.

Roast the foods until they are very soft and tender and allow them to cool slightly before chopping them to a spoonable mash. At this point you can move from a blender to a food processor. The idea is to grind the food but not puree it completely. Here's a sample talk-through recipe to demonstrate how the process works.

ROASTED BROCCOLI WITH PARMESAN AND OLIVE OIL

This is a great example of roasting in action and, again, is more about technique than specific quantities or ratios. By all means, feel free to swap out the broccoli for any vegetables that look good or those that you already know are working for your child.

Preheat your oven to 350°F. Wash one head of organic broccoli. With a sharp knife, separate the florets from the stalk in small pieces, trying to make them uniform in size. Don't waste the stalk! Instead, determine where it gets very woody (usually at the very bottom) and discard only that part; the rest of the stem is perfectly edible. Chop the stalk into pieces the same size as the florets. Scatter the florets and stalk pieces on a rimmed baking sheet in one even layer and drizzle with extra-virgin olive oil. Season the broccoli with a touch of salt. Roast the broccoli for about 15 minutes. You should be able to get a really tasty caramelization in that time, but if the broccoli doesn't feel soft enough to puree, throw it back in for another 5 minutes. It should smell like really good home cooking.

With a spatula, scrape the broccoli into a food processor and either pulse a few times for a coarse texture or turn the food

processor on and let it go for a minute until you get a very fine mash. It's up to you, depending on how well your child is using her new teeth. Play around with it to find the texture that she likes best.

Finish by adding about a teaspoon of freshly grated Parmesan cheese and pulse it one more time to incorporate the cheese. Taste the mixture to see if it needs a little more salt. I also like to add a drop or two of fresh lemon juice.

The broccoli mash is amazing mixed with a little more olive oil and tossed with freshly cooked pasta, so consider scooping out a portion for your baby and serving the rest for yourself and older diners. It's a two-in-one meal for you and your baby. (More on this in the next two stages.)

Adding Protein to Their Diet

Most pediatricians counsel that it's safe to add meat to a child's diet somewhere between 7 and 10 months of age. It's always best to wait until they have a few teeth before introducing the texture of meat, and even then, cooked meats need to be well pureed with vegetables and maybe rice until very smooth. Once they begin to "chew," at 10 to 12 months of age—the same time they begin to use their fingers as tools, picking up Cheerios, for example—it's OK to give them meat chopped up into tiny pieces to eat with very close supervision. This opens up a whole new world of child-and-family-friendly dishes that everyone can enjoy together.

SPINACH AND BANANA PUREE

MAKES FOUR ½-CUP SERVINGS
OR TWO 1-CUP SERVINGS

Bananas are an easy way to sneak superhealthy nutrients into lots of dishes. This bright green puree is amazing—one of my favorites in the book.

12 ounces fresh spinach, well washed
and tough stems removed

2 bananas

¼ cup plain whole-fat yogurt

¼ cup unfiltered apple juice

Combine all the ingredients in a blender or food processor. Puree until smooth.

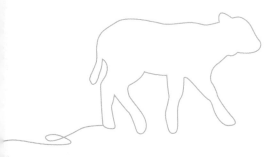

GREEN BEAN, POTATO, AND KALE PUREE

MAKES FOUR ½-CUP SERVINGS
OR TWO 1-CUP SERVINGS

¼ pound green beans

1 large russet (baking) potato, peeled and sliced

4 large kale leaves, stems removed and coarsely chopped

1 cup organic chicken stock

3 tablespoons freshly grated Parmesan cheese

1 tablespoon extra-virgin olive oil

Kale is my go-to ingredient when I'm looking to up the nutritional ante of a baby food. Kale is known as the "Super Green"—it's packed with beta-carotene and vitamins C and K, and it's a really good source of iron. Blended with potatoes, green beans, chicken stock, and Parm, it's not only incredibly healthy, it has a very deep and delicious flavor, like something an Italian grandmother would make.

In a saucepan, combine the beans, potato, kale, and stock and bring to a boil over medium heat. Reduce the heat. Cook uncovered until the potatoes are fork-tender, about 10 minutes.

Transfer the contents of the saucepan to a blender and add the Parmesan and olive oil. Puree until as smooth as you prefer.

Serve warm.

PARSNIP, PEAR, AND FIG PUREE

This tastes like Christmas. I was looking for a puree to serve with a quail dish at my San Francisco restaurant, Wayfare Tavern, and after a few trials I landed on this savory combo. It's crazy good.

In a saucepan, combine the parsnips, pear, and figs. Add ½ cup water and bring to a boil. Reduce to a simmer and cook until the parsnips are tender, about 20 minutes. Let cool slightly.

Transfer the parsnips, pear, and figs along with the cooking liquid to a blender and puree until smooth consistency.

Fold in the orange zest and maple syrup and stir until well blended. Serve warm.

MAKES FOUR ½-CUP SERVINGS
OR TWO 1-CUP SERVINGS

2 medium parsnips, peeled and cut into 1-inch pieces

1 Bosc pear, cored and cut into chunks

3 dried figs

1 teaspoon grated orange zest

2 tablespoons pure maple syrup

BANANA, PINEAPPLE, AND AVOCADO PUDDING

MAKES FOUR ½-CUP SERVINGS
OR TWO 1-CUP SERVINGS

1 banana, sliced

¼ pineapple, peeled, cored, and cut into chunks

½ Hass avocado

½ cup plain whole-milk yogurt

When your child tastes this for the first time, watch as he thinks about it for a second, and then smiles for another bite. None of the ingredients in this smooth pudding are cooked, so it's as easy to put together as a smoothie.

Combine all the ingredients in a blender and puree until smooth. Serve immediately.

CARROT, MANGO, AND APPLE PUREE

Brace yourself for one of the most amazing flavor combinations you'll ever taste. Zip, bang, pow, you won't know what hit you first: the bright orange of the beta-carotene in the carrots, the sweetness of the apples, or the fresh tang of the mango. In all the years I've been cooking, this is one of the best things I've made.

Preheat the oven to 350°F.

Arrange the carrots, mango, and apples on a rimmed baking sheet and roast until the fruit has browned and the carrots are tender, 20 to 25 minutes.

Scrape the fruit and carrots into a blender and puree until smooth.

MAKES THREE ½-CUP SERVINGS

3 medium carrots, peeled

1 mango, cut into chunks

2 medium Granny Smith or Rome apples, halved and cored

ROASTED BANANAS AND BLUEBERRIES

MAKES FOUR ½-CUP SERVINGS
OR TWO 1-CUP SERVINGS

3 large bananas

1 pint blueberries

I learned the secret of roasting bananas when I worked at Charlie Palmer's famous New York restaurant, Aureole, where he would fold roasted bananas into the whipped sweet potatoes. The flavor profile blew my mind and I've been using it ever since. Here I combine the bananas with deep-purple roasted blueberries—all cooked together on one pan. It's so good you'll have to remind yourself to save some for your child, because you'll want to eat it all.

Preheat the oven to 350°F.

Arrange the unpeeled bananas on a rimmed baking sheet and scatter the blueberries around them. Roast until the berries have burst and the banana skins have become a deep brown, 20 to 25 minutes. Let cool slightly.

Peel the bananas and place in a blender. Scrape the blueberries into the food processor and puree with the bananas until smooth.

ROASTED APPLES AND CINNAMON

The flavor of applesauce from a jar just can't compete with homemade. I just did a taste test with my 2-year-old daughter, Dorothy, and when she tasted mine, she closed her eyes, thought about it for a second, and then started to laugh. "Yummy in my tummy," she said. I didn't get that from the boring old store-bought applesauce.

Preheat the oven to 400°F.

Arrange the apples, cut-side down, on a rimmed baking sheet. Roast the apples until tender when pierced with a fork, 20 to 25 minutes.

Transfer the apples to a blender. Add the lemon juice, cinnamon, and salt and pulse the apples until smooth.

MAKES ABOUT THREE ½-CUP SERVINGS

4 large Granny Smith or Rome apples, halved and cored

1 teaspoon fresh lemon juice

½ teaspoon cinnamon

Pinch of salt

ROASTED APPLESAUCE
WITH PLUMS, SWEET SPICE,
AND MAPLE SYRUP

MAKES ABOUT THREE 1-CUP SERVINGS
OR SIX ½-CUP SERVINGS

6 medium apples, halved lengthwise
and cored, peel left on

2 plums, halved lengthwise and pitted

2 tablespoons pure maple syrup

¼ teaspoon ground cinnamon

Pinch grated nutmeg

Roasting apples for applesauce is a really versatile technique and can be switched out with just about any fruit. Peaches look good? You've got an extra pint of blueberries in the fridge? It all works.

Preheat the oven to 400°F.

Arrange the apples and plums, skin-side down, on a rimmed baking sheet. Roast until they look as if they have burst, 30 to 40 minutes.

Remove the baking sheet from the oven and let the fruit cool slightly.

In a food processor, combine the roasted fruit, maple syrup, cinnamon, and nutmeg and process to the desired consistency.

SPINACH AND ROASTED PEARS
WITH PARM

MAKES FOUR ½-CUP SERVINGS
OR TWO 1-CUP SERVINGS

2 Bartlett pears, halved lengthwise
and cored

½ cup organic chicken stock

2 bunches fresh spinach, well washed
and stems removed

2 tablespoons freshly grated
Parmesan cheese

Spinach is at the top of the list as far as nutrient bombs go, with iron, potassium, beta-carotene, and vitamins K and C. Spinach also contains glycoglycerolipids, which have been shown to protect the intestinal lining. That said, not all kids love spinach on its own. Creating a salty/sweet flavor balance with the addition of pear and Parmesan will help your small children clean their bowls. I've also used this puree to sauce fish dishes at my restaurants—it's that good.

Preheat the oven to 400°F.

Arrange the pears, cut-side down, on a rimmed baking sheet. Roast the pears until tender when pierced with a fork, 20 to 25 minutes. Set aside to cool slightly.

Meanwhile, in a large skillet, bring the stock to a boil over medium heat. Add the spinach and cook, stirring, until wilted, 3 to 5 minutes. Remove from the heat and allow to cool, then press the spinach against the side of the pan with a kitchen spoon to remove as much moisture as possible.

Combine the spinach, pears, and Parmesan in a blender and puree until smooth.

ROASTED GOLDEN BEETS AND APRICOTS

This fantastic combination tastes as sunny as it looks. If it's not fresh apricot season, substituting dried apricots, soaked in boiling water for 20 minutes and then drained, works just as well.

Preheat the oven to 400°F.

Arrange the beets and apricots on a rimmed baking sheet and roast until the beets are tender when pierced with a fork, 25 to 30 minutes.

Transfer the beet and apricots to a blender and puree until smooth.

MAKES FOUR ½-CUP SERVINGS
OR TWO 1-CUP SERVINGS

8 medium golden beets, scrubbed and halved lengthwise

8 large fresh apricots, halved lengthwise

ROASTED SUMMER SQUASH
WITH **HERBS**

MAKES FOUR ½-CUP SERVINGS
OR TWO 1-CUP SERVINGS

4 large yellow summer squash,
halved lengthwise

2 tablespoons assorted fresh herbs
such as parsley, thyme, tarragon

1 tablespoon extra-virgin olive oil

Salt and freshly ground pepper

Here's a good way to introduce your baby to savory foods. Roasting squash concentrates and deepens its mild flavor, and a bit of olive oil smooths out the texture of the puree. It's also a great side dish for the rest of the family.

Preheat the oven to 350°F.

Arrange the squash and herbs on a rimmed baking sheet. Drizzle with the oil and season with salt and pepper. Roast the squash until tender when pierced with a fork, 20 to 25 minutes. Remove the pan from the oven and set aside to cool slightly.

Place the roasted squash and herbs in a blender and puree until smooth.

SUMMER SQUASH, YUKON GOLD POTATOES, AND PARMESAN

This recipe is a celebration of summer flavors. Straight from the farmers' market, you can have this put together in about 30 minutes. It also tastes really good as a side dish with pork chops.

Preheat the oven to 400°F.

Arrange the squash, potatoes, and onion in a single layer on a rimmed baking sheet. Top with the thyme leaves and drizzle with the oil.

Roast the vegetables until nicely browned and tender when pierced with a knife, 25 to 30 minutes.

In a food processor, puree all the ingredients to desired consistency.

MAKES FOUR ½-CUP SERVINGS
OR TWO 1-CUP SERVINGS

2 medium summer squash,
cut into 1-inch chunks

½ pound small Yukon Gold potatoes,
well scrubbed, cut into 1-inch chunks

1 medium white onion,
cut into 1-inch chunks

1 teaspoon fresh thyme leaves

1 tablespoon extra-virgin olive oil

2 tablespoons grated Parmesan cheese

STAGE 3
(9–12 months)

FOODS WITH TEXTURE

Braised Beef with
Apples and Roots

TODDLER IN THE KITCHEN

I am a big advocate of letting children play in the kitchen while the grown-ups cook. When our small children were crawling, I would set up a "drum kit" of inverted pots and pans complete with hi-hat crash cymbals of pot lids hanging off the handles. I would then give them two wooden spoons and let the rock show begin. I know what you're thinking: After a long day at work, the last thing you want is open-mike night while you are trying to get dinner on the table. But the point is to make the kitchen a place of enjoyment. Give them something to do that's fun, but within eyeshot so they can watch you (and vice versa). When they start walking, I strongly recommend getting a play stove so they can "cook dinner" right along with you. It's a creative outlet that lets your children role-play what you are doing, and it gives them a sense of shared responsibility—pride even.

My wife bought our kids wooden play fruit that connect in the middle with Velcro, and when they "cut" it with their wooden toy knife, they feel like they are helping and doing something important. They really are doing something important for themselves.

This kitchen play also gives your children the opportunity to see what food looks like *before* it gets cooked, which is an important part of getting them to accept what's on their plate when dinner is served later. They will have a harder time saying "I don't like it" if they watched it being made from scratch. Even helping pick out what's for dinner makes a big difference in ownership.

As children become self-feeders, mastering the art of holding a fork or spoon, it's time to add a new blending technique—one that also happens to be very low tech. "Fork-mashing" the same meal that the rest of the family is having introduces your child to adult food at a very simple level. Just use the tines of a fork to smash the vegetables, starch, and well-cooked meat or other protein together into a blended mash, leaving some identifiable bits and pieces of each element. It's quick, it's easy, and it's a good transition between the smoother, more homogenized purees you've been feeding your child and bigger finger foods. You can also pulse everything together in the food processor for a slightly finer texture, but just pulse the mixture a few times, leaving the texture a bit coarser than their earliest foods.

Which brings me to cooking for your crawler or soon-to-be toddler. It's time to crank up the oven and give those baking sheets a workout, because we're going to be roasting everything. Most of these recipes require only a single pot or baking sheet and will allow you to include your child in what the rest of the family is eating—just divide the entire recipe into adult and kid-friendly portions and pulse or fork-mash as needed. You've never tasted simple cooking like this, and your children—and you—will love it.

ROASTED GOLDEN BEETS
WITH QUINOA AND FETA

MAKES 4 ADULT SERVINGS
OR ABOUT 6 KID SERVINGS

5 small golden beets, scrubbed

3 teaspoons extra-virgin olive oil

Salt and freshly ground pepper

1 cup quinoa

1 ounce fresh spinach, stems removed, shredded

3 tablespoons raisins

3 tablespoons crumbled feta cheese

½ teaspoon fresh lemon juice

Beets and spinach make this salad incredibly nutritious, but it's the addition of quinoa that catapults it into the realm of superfood! This South American grain is just as easy to make as couscous but packs a lot more protein and has a nice toothy crunch. You'll find this salad quite delicious and easy to make, so give it a try, especially if you haven't really played around with quinoa that much.

Preheat the oven to 400°F.

Arrange the beets on a rimmed baking sheet. Drizzle with 1 teaspoon of the olive oil and season with salt and pepper. Roast the beets until tender when pierced with a fork, 25 to 30 minutes. Let the beets stand until cool enough to handle, then use wet hands to slip the skins from the beets. Cut the beets into quarters.

Meanwhile, in a 1½-quart saucepan, bring 2 cups of salted water to a boil. Add the quinoa and cook, stirring occasionally, until all the liquid is absorbed, about 20 minutes. Fold the spinach into the quinoa and set aside.

In a large bowl, fold the quinoa mixture, beets, raisins, and feta together and drizzle with the remaining 2 teaspoons of olive oil and the lemon juice.

Divide the entire recipe into both adult and child-friendly portions. For adults, serve as is. For children, transfer to a food processor and puree or fork-mash, as appropriate.

PEARLED COUSCOUS WITH BRUSSELS SPROUTS AND CHICKPEAS

This is one of the simplest dishes in the book. Pearled couscous, also called Israeli couscous, can be found in most grocery stories. It's easy to make and can be used as a base for lots of on-the-fly salads.

In a 1½-quart saucepan, bring 1¾ cups water to a boil over medium heat. Add the couscous, stir, reduce the heat, and cook uncovered until all the liquid has been absorbed, 5 to 7 minutes. Set aside.

In a large skillet, cook the bacon over medium-high heat until most of the fat has been rendered, about 5 minutes. Add the Brussels sprouts and cook, stirring occasionally, until the bacon is crisp and the Brussels sprouts have softened, 5 to 7 minutes longer. Fold in the chickpeas and couscous and stir to combine.

Divide into adult and child-friendly portions. Pulse the kid portions in the food processor or fork-mash to the appropriate texture. Serve warm sprinkled with the Parmesan cheese.

MAKES 2 ADULT SERVINGS
OR 4 KID SERVINGS

1 box (4.7 ounces) pearled
or Israeli couscous

2 slices thick-cut bacon, cut crosswise
into 1-inch pieces

½ pound Brussels sprouts, cut into
thin wedges

½ cup canned chickpeas,
rinsed and drained

2 tablespoons grated
Parmesan cheese

CHICKEN AND KALE RISOTTO WITH PINE NUTS AND BACON

This deeply delicious dish sounds complicated, but it's really easy to make and the mushy, homey texture will put a huge smile on your child's face.

Preheat the oven to 350°F. Line a rimmed baking sheet with parchment paper.

Arrange the chicken on the baking sheet, drizzle with olive oil, and season with salt and pepper. Bake for 20 minutes, then add the kale, onion, bacon, and pine nuts to the same baking sheet, return to the oven, and bake until the bacon is crisp and the chicken has reached an internal temperature of 155°F when tested with an instant-read thermometer, 10 to 15 minutes. Keep warm.

Meanwhile, bring the stock to a simmer in a large pot over medium heat; keep warm.

In a large saucepan, melt the butter over medium heat. Add the rice and stir to coat with the butter. Cook, stirring occasionally, until opaque, 2 to 3 minutes.

Add ½ cup of the hot stock to the rice and cook, stirring constantly until all the stock is absorbed. Continue adding stock ½ cup at a time and stirring constantly until the rice is creamy and tender. Keep warm.

Transfer the chicken, kale, onion, bacon, and pine nuts to a food processor and pulse on and off just until coarsely chopped. Fold into the rice and serve warm.

MAKES 4 TO 6 ADULT SERVINGS
OR 8 TO 10 KID SERVINGS

2 boneless, skinless chicken breast halves (about 6 ounces each)

Extra-virgin olive oil

Salt and freshly ground pepper

2 or 3 large kale leaves, ribs removed, torn into 1-inch pieces

1 small yellow onion, cut into wedges, layers separated

1 slice thick-cut bacon, cut into 1-inch pieces

3 tablespoons pine nuts

4 cups organic chicken stock

2 tablespoons unsalted butter

1 cup Arborio rice

CHICKEN WITH WHITE RICE, BROCCOLI, CARROTS, AND PEAS

MAKES 2 TO 4 ADULT SERVINGS
OR 6 TO 8 KID SERVINGS

2 tablespoons extra-virgin olive oil

2 boneless, skinless chicken breast halves (about 4 ounces each)

1 cup broccoli florets (include some of the green leaves if you like)

2 carrots

1 small yellow onion, cut into rings

½ cup sugar snap peas

½ cup frozen green peas

1 tablespoon unsalted butter

1½ cups long-grain white rice

3 cups organic chicken stock

My kids love really simple, wholesome, delicious dishes, and this is a good one. Like a lot of the recipes in the book, it all cooks up together in one roasting pan that goes from stovetop to oven, old-school casserole-style. Change the vegetables up with whatever you find at the farmers' market.

Preheat the oven to 375°F.

In a small roasting pan, heat the oil over medium heat until shimmering. Add the chicken and cook, turning once, until browned, 7 to 10 minutes.

Add the broccoli, carrots, onion, sugar snaps, and peas and cook until the vegetables are bright in color, 3 to 5 minutes. Transfer the chicken and vegetables to a plate and set aside.

Add the butter to the same pan and return to medium heat. Once the butter is melted, add the rice and stir until coated. Add the stock and bring to a boil over medium-high heat. Arrange the chicken and vegetables on top of the rice and place the pan in the oven.

Bake uncovered until the chicken has reached an internal temperature of 165°F and the rice has absorbed the liquid, 30 to 40 minutes.

Divide the dish into adult and child-friendly portions. Roughly chop the child portions and transfer to a food processor. Pulse on and off until coarsely or finely chopped, as desired.

GINGER CHICKEN
WITH COCONUT

I love the bright flavors of Thai food and find that many children are also partial to the mild sweet/sour accents of coconut, ginger, and lime you find in many Thai dishes. The chicken and rice cook together in one pan, allowing the flavors to meld as they bake.

Preheat the oven to 400°F.

In a heavy roasting pan, heat the olive oil over medium heat until shimmering. Season the chicken with salt and pepper and brown lightly on both sides, 5 to 7 minutes. Transfer to a plate and set aside.

Add the onion and ginger to the pan and cook until the onion is translucent, 3 to 5 minutes. Pour the coconut milk and stock into the pan and bring to a boil.

Add the rice and cook until some of the liquid has been absorbed by the rice, 5 to 7 minutes. Arrange the chicken on top of the rice and sprinkle with the coconut.

Bake until the chicken has reached an internal temperature of 165°F and the rice is tender, 20 to 25 minutes. There should be some liquid remaining in the pan. Sprinkle with the cilantro and squeeze the lime halves over all.

Divide the recipe into as many adult and child-friendly portions as needed. Roughly chop the child portions and transfer to a food processor. Pulse on and off until coarsely or finely chopped, as desired.

MAKES 4 ADULT SERVINGS
OR 6 TO 8 KID SERVINGS

2 tablespoons extra-virgin olive oil

4 boneless, skinless chicken thighs, rinsed well and patted dry

Salt and freshly ground pepper

1 small yellow onion, finely chopped

2 tablespoons minced fresh ginger

1 can (13.5 ounces) coconut milk

1½ cups organic chicken stock

1½ cups long-grain white rice

½ cup unsweetened shredded coconut

2 tablespoons fresh cilantro leaves

1 lime, halved

ROAST TURKEY WITH SWEET POTATO, BROWN RICE, AND CRANBERRIES

MAKES 6 TO 8 ADULT SERVINGS
OR 12 KID SERVINGS

1 pound boneless turkey breast

1 large sweet potato, scrubbed and halved lengthwise

½ cup fresh cranberries

1 small yellow onion, quartered, layers separated

6 fresh sage leaves

3 tablespoons extra-virgin olive oil

Salt and freshly ground pepper

1 cup cooked brown rice, warm or at room temperature

How great is the idea of a complete Thanksgiving feast all roasted together on a single baking sheet? The flavors are bright and satisfying and the cooking technique is pretty cool. I'm not saying this will replace how you prepare your holiday spread—but then again, it just might. My kids love this dish; it makes a Tuesday night feel like a holiday.

Preheat the oven to 400°F.

Arrange the turkey, sweet potato, cranberries, and onion on a rimmed baking sheet and scatter the sage leaves on top. Drizzle with 1 tablespoon of the oil and season with salt and pepper.

Roast uncovered for 25 to 30 minutes, or until the turkey has reached an internal temperature of 155°F when tested at its thickest point with an instant-read thermometer. Let the turkey rest for 10 minutes.

Divide the meal into adult and child-friendly portions. For the kid portions, shred the turkey into small pieces and scoop the sweet potato flesh from the skin. Place in a food processor along with some of the cranberries, onion, and sage. Add a few tablespoons of brown rice. Drizzle in the remaining 2 tablespoons of oil and pulse on and off until coarsely chopped. Serve warm.

ROAST TURKEY WITH HERBED VEGETABLES

MAKES 4 TO 6 ADULT SERVINGS
OR 6 TO 8 KID SERVINGS

1 boneless turkey breast half
(about 2 pounds)

Salt and freshly ground pepper

1 bunch baby turnips,
scrubbed, trimmed, and halved

1 bunch baby carrots,
scrubbed and trimmed

6 ounces small red or Yukon Gold
potatoes, scrubbed and halved

1 cup pearl onions, peeled

1 cup frozen green peas

3 sprigs thyme

Extra-virgin olive oil

Another complete and balanced meal that is cooked together in a single pan. Pulse this to the appropriate texture in a food processor and you have a delicious home-cooked dish for your toddler, and a simple, satisfying dinner for the rest of the family. If you can't find baby carrots and turnips, quarter 2 or 3 larger ones.

Preheat the oven to 400°F.

Season both sides of the turkey breast with salt and pepper and place in a roasting pan. Arrange the turnips, carrots, potatoes, onions, peas, and thyme around the turkey and drizzle with olive oil.

Roast uncovered until the turkey has reached an internal temperature of 165°F when tested at its thickest point with an instant-read thermometer, 35 to 40 minutes.

Let stand for 5 minutes, then divide into both adult and child-friendly portions. Roughly chop the child portions and transfer to a food processor. Pulse on and off until coarsely or finely chopped, as desired.

ROASTED SALMON WITH GREEN PEA RISOTTO

Getting kids to eat things that are green can be a challenge, but if you start early enough, broccoli, green beans, asparagus, spinach, and yes, even peas, can easily become lifelong favorites. My older son, Miles, loves this dish, and I've been making it for him since he could sit in a high chair.

Preheat the oven to 400°F.

In a large ovenproof skillet, heat the oil over medium-high heat. Add the salmon pieces and cook without turning until browned on the bottom, 2 to 3 minutes. Transfer the pan to the oven and cook until the salmon just flakes when tested with a fork, about 10 minutes.

In a large saucepan, bring the broth to a boil over medium heat. Add the peas, reduce the heat, and cook until bright green, 1 to 2 minutes. With a strainer, scoop the peas into a bowl. Transfer half of the peas to a blender and puree until smooth; set aside. Keep the broth warm.

In a large saucepan, toast the rice over medium heat, stirring often, until the rice has darkened slightly and has a nutty aroma, 3 to 5 minutes. Add the broth 1 cup at a time, waiting until each addition is almost absorbed before adding more and stirring the rice frequently.

Before all the liquid has been absorbed, stir in both the pureed and whole peas, butter, and cheese. Serve the salmon fillets atop the risotto, or flake the salmon into small pieces and stir into the risotto for child portions.

MAKES 4 ADULT SERVINGS
OR 6 TO 8 KID SERVINGS

2 tablespoons extra-virgin olive oil

1 pound skinless wild salmon fillet,
any bones removed,
cut into 4 equal portions

4 cups organic chicken or
vegetable broth

1 cup frozen green peas

1 cup Arborio rice

1 tablespoon unsalted butter

½ cup grated Parmesan cheese

MAPLE ROASTED PORK CHOPS WITH BUTTERNUT SQUASH AND BEETS

When I came up with this recipe, my food stylist bet me that there was no way a sliver of butternut squash and a split beet could cook in the same amount of time as a pork chop, but I insisted that we had to make it easy for parents to get dinner on the table. One baking sheet, that's it. And guess what? It worked like a charm. Now to be fair, my pork chops were a substantial 6 ounces each; if you buy smaller chops, give the butternut squash and beets a 10-minute head start.

Preheat the oven to 400°F.

Season the pork chops with salt and pepper and arrange them with the squash, cut-side down, in a single layer on a rimmed baking sheet. Add the beets, onion, and rosemary branches to the baking sheet and drizzle everything with the maple syrup and olive oil.

Roast the meat and veggies until the pork chops are crisp around the edges and their centers are still slightly pink (with an internal temperature of 155°F), 25 to 30 minutes.

Divide the meat and vegetables into as many adult and child-friendly portions as needed. Roughly chop the child portions and place in a food processor. Pulse until coarsely or finely chopped, as desired.

MAKES 4 ADULT SERVINGS
OR 6 TO 8 KID SERVINGS

4 boneless pork chops
(4 to 6 ounces each)

Salt and freshly ground pepper

1 medium butternut squash
(about 1½ pounds), halved
lengthwise and seeded

6 small yellow beets, scrubbed

1 small yellow onion, cut into wedges

2 sprigs rosemary

¼ cup pure maple syrup

2 tablespoons extra-virgin olive oil

BRAISED BEEF WITH APPLES AND ROOTS

MAKES 4 TO 6 ADULT SERVINGS
OR ABOUT 8 KID SERVINGS

2 tablespoons extra-virgin olive oil

1 pound beef shoulder, trimmed and cut into four equal pieces

Salt and freshly ground pepper

6 whole baby carrots, scrubbed

2 parsnips, scrubbed and sliced ½-inch thick

1 golden beet, scrubbed and cut into wedges

1 Rome apple, cut into wedges and seeds removed

1 sprig rosemary

2 cups beef stock

1 cup apple juice

No one uses pressure cookers anymore, which is a shame because they are a supereasy and quick way to give foods the soft texture and deep-braised flavor that takes hours to achieve with conventional cooking methods. Using a pressure cooker, this family favorite cooks in just 20 minutes (though I've also included the regular stovetop cooking procedure for those who prefer it). The meltingly tender meat and vegetables lend themselves well to fork-mashing rather than chopping or pureeing.

Pressure cooker method: In a pressure cooker, heat the oil over medium heat until shimmering, 2 to 3 minutes. Add the beef, season with salt and pepper, and cook, turning often, until the edges are beginning to brown, 5 to 7 minutes.

Add the carrots, parsnips, beet, apple, rosemary, beef stock, and apple juice to the pot. Fasten the lid securely and bring up to full pressure over medium-high heat. Reduce heat to medium and cook for 25 minutes.

Remove the cooker from the heat and release the steam valve. Carefully remove the lid and let the meat and vegetables stand for 5 to 10 minutes.

Conventional method: In a large deep pot, heat the oil over medium heat until shimmering, 2 to 3 minutes. Add the beef, season with salt and pepper, and cook, turning often, until the edges are beginning to brown, 5 to 7 minutes.

Add the carrots, parsnips, beet, apple, rosemary, beef stock, and apple juice. Cover and cook over medium heat until the meat is tender and vegetables have softened, about 2½ hours.

Remove the pot from the heat and let stand for 5 minutes.

Divide the entire recipe into both adult and child-friendly portions. For adults, serve the beef and vegetables with some of the cooking liquid spooned over. For older kids, chop the meat and vegetables into small bite-size pieces, or transfer to a food processor and pulse on and off, adding some of the cooking liquid as needed.

NY STRIP WITH ASIAN VEGETABLES

Chinese food is one of those universally appealing cuisines and a great place to start introducing your children to international flavors. This is a delicious, from-scratch version of a beef-and-vegetable stir-fry; pulse it together with some rice to make a finer texture for new teeth.

MAKES 4 ADULT SERVINGS
OR 6 TO 8 KID SERVINGS

2 tablespoons olive oil

1 pound NY strip steak
(also called club steak), cut into
¼-inch-thick slices

1 cup small broccoli florets

1 medium carrot, cut into matchsticks

1 cup snow peas, slivered lengthwise

1 piece (1 inch) fresh ginger,
coarsely chopped

1 cup beef broth

½ teaspoon cornstarch

4-ounce can whole water chestnuts,
drained and halved

½ teaspoon toasted sesame oil

1 cup cooked white rice

In a large wok or skillet, heat the olive oil over medium-high heat. When it's very hot, add the steak and cook, stirring often, until the meat is browned and starting to become crisp around the edges, about 5 minutes. Leaving the oil in the pan, transfer the steak to a bowl.

Add the broccoli, carrot, snow peas, and ginger to the pan and cook, stirring occasionally, until tender, 5 to 7 minutes. Add the vegetables to the bowl with the steak.

In a small cup, mix ¼ cup of the broth and the cornstarch and stir until well blended. Add the broth mixture to the pan and stir until smooth, then add the remaining ¾ cup broth and the water chestnuts. Cook until the sauce has reduced slightly, 3 to 5 minutes. Return the beef and vegetables to the pan and stir to coat with the sauce. Season with the sesame oil.

Divide the recipe into adult and child-friendly portions. Pulse each kid portion in the food processor with a few tablespoons of white rice until as fine or as coarse as your baby prefers. Serve adult portions over white rice.

CAULIFLOWER GRATIN

MAKES 6 TO 8 SERVINGS
FOR ADULTS OR KIDS

2 tablespoons extra-virgin olive oil

½ medium yellow onion, cut into
8 wedges

1 head cauliflower, leaves and stem
left intact, coarsely chopped

2 sprigs thyme

1 tablespoon unbleached
all-purpose flour

¼ teaspoon freshly grated nutmeg

½ cup whole milk

4 ounces fresh mozzarella, diced

¼ cup freshly grated Parmesan cheese

½ cup panko breadcrumbs

The unsung hero of the vegetable world finally takes a stand in this cheesy, comforting gratin. I love not only the flavor, but the way it fills the house with its savory, roasted aroma. Great pureed, fork-mashed, or as a side dish your children will love for years to come.

Preheat the oven to 425°F.

In a 12-inch ovenproof skillet, heat the olive oil over medium heat. Add the onion and cook, stirring often, until the onion has browned, 5 to 7 minutes. Add the cauliflower and thyme and cook until the cauliflower has browned slightly, 8 to 10 minutes.

Sprinkle the flour and nutmeg over the cauliflower. Pour the milk in and continue to cook, stirring occasionally, until the sauce thickens slightly, about 5 minutes. Sprinkle evenly with the mozzarella, then top with the Parmesan and panko. (The gratin can be prepared to this point up to 2 days in advance and stored tightly covered in the refrigerator.)

Bake the gratin uncovered on the middle rack of the oven until the cheese is bubbling and the breadcrumbs are toasted, 7 to 10 minutes. Remove from the oven, cover loosely with foil, and let stand for 10 minutes before serving.

Divide the gratin into as many adult and child-friendly portions as needed. Transfer the child portions to a food processor and pulse until coarsely or finely chopped, as desired.

BAKED APPLES
AND BARLEY

MAKES 4 TO 6 ADULT SERVINGS
OR 6 TO 8 KID SERVINGS

2 Rome or Granny Smith apples, cut into wedges

1 cup blueberries

1 cup cooked pearled barley (see Note)

½ cup sliced almonds

3 tablespoons unsalted butter, at room temperature

2 tablespoons brown sugar

1 tablespoon ground flaxseed

1 teaspoon pure vanilla extract

½ teaspoon ground cinnamon

Pinch of salt

½ cup instant oatmeal

This is a really simple and healthy fruit crumble. Cooking the barley first gives the crumble a delicious crunch. I've also dusted the top with uncooked instant oatmeal, which absorbs the bubbling berry juices.

Preheat the oven to 375°F. Line a rimmed baking sheet with parchment paper.

Arrange the apples and blueberries on the baking sheet. In a large bowl, combine the barley, almonds, butter, brown sugar, flaxseed, vanilla, cinnamon, and salt and stir until well mixed. Spoon the barley mixture evenly over the apples and blueberries, then sprinkle with the oatmeal.

Bake until the blueberries have burst and the barley and almonds are lightly browned, 25 to 30 minutes. Allow to cool for a minute or two, then transfer the child portions to a food processor and puree until smooth. Serve warm.

Note: To cook barley, place ½ cup raw barley in a saucepan with 2 cups of water. Bring to a boil, cover, and reduce the heat to a simmer. Cook the barley until tender but not mushy, 40 to 50 minutes.

GRAIN AND BERRY RISOTTO

This "risotto" is basically rice pudding made better with whole grains and a very small amount of butter. The rice gets "creamed" out risotto-style at the very end. I know . . . it's clever.

In a large saucepan, bring the apple juice to a boil. Add the rice blend, cover, and reduce the heat to a simmer. Cook until the rice is tender and all of the juice is absorbed, 40 to 45 minutes. Check the pan after 30 minutes and add a bit more juice if needed.

Add the butter to the rice and stir until combined, then add the berries. Continue to cook over medium heat until some of the berries have burst, 2 to 3 minutes. Remove the pan from the heat.

Divide the entire recipe into both adult and child-friendly portions. Puree the child portions in a food processor until nearly smooth.

Serve warm with a dollop of applesauce and a sprinkle of cinnamon.

MAKES 4 TO 6 ADULT SERVINGS
OR 6 TO 8 KID SERVINGS

4 cups apple juice

1 cup wild rice blend

2 tablespoons unsalted butter

1 cup assorted berries (blackberries, raspberries, blueberries)

½ cup unsweetened applesauce

⅛ teaspoon ground cinnamon

PEACH RICE PUDDING

MAKES 4 ADULT SERVINGS
OR 6 TO 8 KID SERVINGS

1 tablespoon unsalted butter

3 ripe peaches, cut into chunks

1 cup long-grain white rice

2 cups apple juice

1 cup whole milk

½ cup coconut milk

1 cinnamon stick

1 teaspoon pure vanilla extract

Pinch of salt

2 tablespoons sugar

When peaches are in season, I really don't think there is a better fruit on earth. Packed with natural sugar from the peaches and carbohydrates from the rice, this healthy energy bomb will keep your children happy and on the playground all day.

In a large saucepan, melt the butter over medium heat until bubbling. Add the peaches and cook until they have released some of their juices, about 5 minutes.

Add the rice and stir until well coated. Add the apple juice, milk, coconut milk, cinnamon stick, vanilla, and salt and bring to a boil. Reduce the heat to medium, cover, and cook until the rice is tender and most of the liquid has been absorbed, about 20 minutes.

Discard the cinnamon stick, fold in the sugar, and stir until well blended. Serve warm or cold.

EVERYONE TO THE TABLE

Quick Sourdough Pizza

After a year of age, the sky's really the limit as far as what children can eat. It's a critical juncture in your child's relationship to food that will shape his eating habits for a long time to come.

It's also an important time to get them used to eating as part of the family and not just the cute little science experiment they've been for the last 6 months or so. The family that eats together not only stays together but creates healthier children. A fascinating 2007 study conducted by the University of Minnesota in conjunction with the American Dietetic Association concluded after interviewing more than 1,500 students—once in high school, then again when they were 20—that eating as a family resulted in adults who ate more fruit, dark green and orange vegetables, and drank fewer soft drinks. Other studies have shown children who eat together with their families on a regular basis have better language skills, get higher grades, and are less likely to experiment with alcohol and drugs. That precious time sitting around the table sharing a meal can absolutely shape the outcome of your children's adult years.

It's a simple idea. Share meals together, and ensure that those meals are full of fresh flavors and interesting textures and colors. It's up to us as parents to guide our children in life. Children need to eat real food, and we have to make better decisions about their nutritional well-being, teaching them to enjoy and appreciate the foods that are really good for them.

You'll love the recipes in this chapter. All of them can be served to the whole family, are very delicious, and are easy to make.

So get in the kitchen and help your children START FRESH.

HORCHATA

Shopping for food in California, you can't help but appreciate the Mexican heritage found in the food products and ingredients at both conventional grocery stores and farmers' markets. Horchata is a healthy rice drink traditionally made by soaking white rice with water, sugar, and Mexican cinnamon overnight until the rice swells and softens. The mixture is pureed and served chilled. I've made this drink both healthier and more delicious by substituting almond milk for water and using brown rice. Depending on the type of brown rice and thickness of its bran layer, soaking times might vary. You can't oversoak the rice, so if it still feels firm after a few hours, just throw it in the fridge overnight. Puree, strain, and serve chilled. It's a great way to start the day.

In a large heatproof bowl, stir together the brown rice, whole almonds, cinnamon stick, pomegranate seeds, and lime zest. Bring the almond milk to a boil in a saucepan over medium heat. Pour the hot almond milk over the rice mixture and stir to combine. Cover and chill for at least 4 hours and preferably overnight; the rice should be very soft.

To serve, pour the mixture into a food processor. Add 1 tablespoon agave syrup and puree until smooth. Taste and add more agave if you'd like. Strain the mixture through a fine-mesh sieve and serve.

MAKES 4 CUPS

1 cup brown rice

1 cup whole skin-on almonds

1-inch piece of cinnamon stick

2 tablespoons pomegranate seeds

Zest of 1 lime, cut into 1-inch strips

4 cups almond milk

Agave syrup

SWEET POTATO AND BLUEBERRY PANCAKES

MAKES ABOUT TWELVE 4-INCH
PANCAKES

2 cups unbleached all-purpose flour

¼ cup sugar

2 teaspoons baking powder

½ teaspoon baking soda

Pinch of salt

3 eggs

2 cups buttermilk

1½ cups sweet potato puree
(page 21)

2 tablespoons unsalted butter, melted

½ teaspoon pure vanilla extract

Vegetable oil, for greasing the skillet

½ cup blueberries

Pure maple syrup and butter,
for serving

Unlike your garden-variety pancakes, these combine great flavor with a healthy dose of nutrients. Versatile sweet potatoes are packed with beta-carotene and vitamins C and E and are a perfect ingredient to work into other dishes because they puree so beautifully. The moisture level in a sweet potato will vary depending on its age, so test out your batter by making a small pancake and add a few tablespoons of flour if it feels too thin.

Preheat the oven to 200°F.

In a large bowl, whisk together the flour, sugar, baking powder, baking soda, and salt until well blended. In another bowl, combine the eggs, buttermilk, melted butter, and vanilla and whisk until well blended.

Stir the buttermilk mixture into the flour mixture, mixing just until combined. Stir in the sweet potato puree.

Heat a large skillet over medium heat and oil lightly. Ladle the batter into the skillet by the ¼ cupful and dot each pancake with a few of the blueberries. Cook until bubbles rise to the surface of the pancakes, 2 to 3 minutes. Flip the pancakes and continue to cook until golden on the second side, another 2 minutes. Transfer to the oven to keep warm while you make the rest of the pancakes.

Serve the pancakes hot with syrup and butter.

ALMOND OATMEAL
WITH ROASTED GRAPES

I've been playing around with almond milk at home a lot lately—not just because of the health benefits of zero grams of saturated fat, tons of vitamin E, and magnesium (which helps your body turn food into energy), but because it's delicious. We often make our own almond milk and I love it, but there are also some good commercial products out there.

Preheat the oven to 250°F. Spread the almonds in a single layer on one rimmed baking sheet and the grapes on a second rimmed baking sheet. Place both sheets in the oven.

Toast the almonds, shaking the pan once about halfway through, until lightly browned, 12 to 15 minutes. Transfer to a bowl to cool. Roast the grapes until they have wrinkled and released some of their juices but are still intact, about 1 hour. Allow to cool on the baking sheet. Coarsely chop the almonds.

In a saucepan, bring the almond milk to a simmer over medium heat. Stir in the oats, reduce the heat to medium, and cook until the oats are cooked and most of the liquid has been absorbed, 10 to 12 minutes.

Ladle the oatmeal into serving bowls and top with the grapes, the chopped almonds, and a sprinkle of brown sugar.

MAKES 4 ADULT SERVINGS
OR 6 TO 8 KID SERVINGS

½ cup whole almonds

2 cups red and green grapes

4 cups almond milk, store-bought or homemade (recipe follows)

2 cups old-fashioned rolled oats

2 tablespoons light brown sugar

1. Soak almonds and a cinnamon stick in water to cover overnight.

2. Transfer almonds, cinnamon stick, and soaking liquid to a blender.

3. Puree until completely smooth.

4. Pour into a nut-milk bag set inside a pitcher.

5. Press to strain out the solids.

6. Chill the almond milk until cold.

HOMEMADE ALMOND MILK

BANANA BREAKFAST SANDWICHES

MAKES 2 ADULT SERVINGS
OR 4 KID SERVINGS

Part French toast, part panini, all delicious, this works as well for a snack as it does for breakfast.

2 bananas, halved crosswise and then halved lengthwise

4 slices whole wheat or multigrain bread

2 eggs

½ cup whole milk

½ teaspoon pure vanilla extract

½ teaspoon ground cinnamon

Pinch of salt

1 tablespoon unsalted butter

2 tablespoons honey

1 teaspoon confectioners' sugar

Arrange the banana slices in a single layer on 2 of the bread slices. Top with the remaining bread slices.

In a large bowl, combine the eggs, milk, vanilla, cinnamon, and salt and whisk to blend. Soak each sandwich in the egg mixture for a minute or two or until the bread is just saturated.

Melt the butter in a large skillet over medium heat. Place the sandwiches in the pan and cook until the bottoms are golden, 2 to 3 minutes. Flip the sandwiches, place a heavy pan on top of the sandwiches to press them, and cook until crisp and golden, 2 to 3 minutes.

Cut each sandwich into quarters and serve warm with a drizzle of honey and a shake of confectioners' sugar.

GOLDFISH CHOWDER

MAKES 4 ADULT SERVINGS
OR 8 KID SERVINGS

1 tablespoon extra-virgin olive oil

2 baby carrots, peeled and cut crosswise into ¼-inch-thick slices

6 ounces assorted new potatoes, scrubbed and chopped

½ small yellow onion, finely chopped

1 slice thick-cut bacon, coarsely chopped

1 bay leaf

2 teaspoons fresh thyme leaves

1 tablespoon unbleached all-purpose flour

½ cup organic chicken stock

1 cup whole milk

1 pound wild cod fillet, skinned and cut into strips

½ cup plain goldfish crackers

I couldn't decide what to call this dish until I reached for our stash of goldfish and thought about using them as "chowder crackers." You've got to admit from time to time we, as parents, tell little fibs to get our children to eat their dinner—like the time I told my oldest son, Miles, that tuna rolls from the sushi restaurant were chicken. He ate all six pieces.

In a large saucepan, heat the oil over medium-high heat until shimmering. Add the carrots, potatoes, onion, bacon, bay leaf, and thyme and cook, stirring, until the bacon is crisp and the potatoes have softened, 5 to 7 minutes.

Sprinkle with the flour and continue to stir until the ingredients are well coated. Add the stock and milk all at once and cook until the broth has thickened, 5 to 7 minutes. Add the fish and continue cook, stirring, until the fish is opaque and starting to flake, about 5 minutes. Discard the bay leaf.

Ladle the warm chowder into bowls and garnish each serving with the goldfish.

MINESTRONE

Traveling through Italy as a young chef, I was often struck by how many of the foods—from polenta and risotto to ragùs and brothy soups—were so cooked down and soft in texture, yet had really deep flavors. Truly beautiful cooking and perfect for very young eaters. This is a great recipe to make and freeze, as it reheats brilliantly. It's delicious pureed as well as fork-mashed for small teeth.

Rinse the beans well and place in a large bowl with water to cover by at least 2 inches. Soak for at least 3 hours and preferably overnight.

The next day, drain the beans and place in a large pot. Add water to cover by an inch or so and bring to a boil over medium-high heat. Reduce the heat to a simmer and add the salt. Cook the beans uncovered, skimming any foam that rises to the surface, until tender, about 1 hour.

Drain the beans and return to the pot. Add the stock, tomatoes, onion, lemon, garlic, rosemary, and bay leaves and bring to a boil. Add the pasta and kale, reduce to a simmer, and cook until the pasta is tender, about 10 minutes. Season with salt and pepper.

If desired, ladle one or more child portions into a food processor and pulse until coarsely or finely chopped.

Serve topped with a sprinkle of Parmesan cheese and a drizzle of olive oil.

MAKES 6 TO 8 ADULT SERVINGS
OR ABOUT 10 KID SERVINGS

2 cups assorted dried beans, such as kidney, great Northern, cannellini, pinto, or navy

Salt

4 cups organic chicken stock

1 can (28 ounces) whole tomatoes, drained

1 medium yellow onion, finely chopped

1 lemon slice (¼ inch)

1 garlic clove, minced

1 sprig rosemary

3 bay leaves

1 cup tubetti or ditalini pasta

5 large kale leaves, stems removed, torn into 1-inch pieces

Freshly ground pepper

Freshly grated Parmesan cheese

Extra-virgin olive oil

SPLIT PEA SOUP WITH BACON AND SWEET POTATOES

My children really love soup and this one is amazing. The peas cook in just water, so seasoning the finished soup is really important. Olive oil, salt, and maybe a touch of fresh lemon juice are all the support the soup base needs to have an incredible, clean flavor. The garnish is chunky and toothsome, perfect for little spoons.

MAKES 4 TO 6 ADULT SERVINGS
OR 6 TO 8 KID SERVINGS

1 medium sweet potato, peeled and cut into ½-inch chunks

2 slices thick-cut bacon, cut crosswise into ½-inch pieces

1 pound dried split peas

1 teaspoon fresh thyme leaves

¼ cup freshly grated Parmesan cheese

Preheat the oven to 400°F.

Arrange the sweet potato and bacon in a single layer on a rimmed baking sheet. Roast the potato and bacon, turning once, until the potato is golden and the bacon is crisp, 20 to 25 minutes.

In a large saucepan, combine the peas and 4 cups water. Bring to a boil over high heat, reduce to a simmer and cook, uncovered, until the peas have softened considerably, 50 minutes to 1 hour. Transfer half the peas and 1 cup of the cooking liquid to a food processor and puree until smooth. Return the puree to the pot and stir to combine.

Ladle into bowls and top each serving with some of the bacon and potato or stir them into the soup. Serve with a sprinkling of the thyme leaves and Parmesan.

TURKEY TORTILLA SOUP

MAKES 8 ADULT SERVINGS
OR 10 TO 12 KID SERVINGS

1 boneless turkey breast half, about 2 pounds, washed and patted dry and cut in half crosswise

1 cup long-grain white rice

1 small yellow onion, finely chopped

4 small tomatoes, cut into wedges

2 small carrots, cut into ¼-inch slices

¼ cup coarsely chopped fresh cilantro

1 garlic clove, sliced

½ teaspoon mild chili powder

2 corn tortillas (6 inch), cut into strips

½ avocado, cut into ¼-inch dice

1 lime

Tortilla soup is the Latin American answer to chicken noodle soup. Pulse ½ cup in the food processor to smooth out the texture and you've got your child's first introduction to the flavors of Mexico—flavors I consider as essential to North American cuisine as Italian ingredients are to Europe. Try to find really mild chili powder so there are no surprises when it comes to the heat.

Preheat the oven to 400°F.

In a stockpot, combine the turkey, rice, onion, tomatoes, carrot, cilantro, garlic, and chili powder. Add 6 cups water and bring to a simmer over medium heat. Cook, stirring occasionally, until the rice and vegetables are tender, about 40 minutes. Remove the turkey from the soup and let cool slightly. When cool enough to handle, shred the turkey with a fork into bite-size pieces and add back into the soup.

While the soup simmers, arrange the tortilla strips on an ungreased baking sheet. Bake until crisp and slightly browned, 4 to 6 minutes.

Ladle as many child portions as needed into a food processor and add a few tortilla strips and avocado cubes for each portion. Puree until nearly smooth.

Serve the soup warm with a squeeze of lime juice. Garnish adult portions with the tortillas strips and avocado.

QUICK SOURDOUGH PIZZA

Kids love pizza and, frankly, so do I—*good* pizza that is. Instead of throwing a frozen pie in the oven, try this quickly assembled bread pizza topped with oven-roasted tomatoes. The roasted tomatoes also make a perfect, quick sauce to toss with pasta.

Preheat the oven to 350°F.

Arrange the tomatoes on a rimmed baking sheet. Top with the onion and drizzle with olive oil. Season with salt and pepper. Roast the tomatoes until they burst and are brown around the edges, 25 to 30 minutes.

When the tomatoes have roasted for 20 minutes, rub the cut sides of the bread loaf with the garlic clove. Place the bread, cut-side up, on another baking sheet and toast until golden, 5 to 7 minutes. Remove from the oven but leave the oven on.

Spoon the tomato mixture onto the toasted bread halves and sprinkle evenly with the mozzarella. Return the loaves to the oven and bake until the cheese is browned and bubbling, 7 to 10 minutes.

Sprinkle each pizza with the basil and fennel fronds (if using), drizzle with some more olive oil, and cut into slices.

MAKES 4 TO 6 ADULT SERVINGS
OR 8 KID SERVINGS

1 pint assorted cherry or small tomatoes, halved lengthwise if larger

1 medium yellow onion, chopped

Extra-virgin olive oil

Salt and freshly ground pepper

1 loaf sourdough Italian bread, halved lengthwise

1 garlic clove, peeled and halved

4 ounces fresh mozzarella cheese, shredded

10 fresh basil leaves, torn into small pieces

Fennel fronds, for garnish (optional)

BUTTERNUT SQUASH MACARONI AND CHEESE

MAKES 4 TO 6 ADULT SERVINGS
OR 8 KID SERVINGS

1 medium (1 to 1½ pounds) butternut squash, halved lengthwise, seeds removed

1 tablespoon extra-virgin olive oil

Salt and freshly ground pepper

12 ounces small pasta shells

½ cup whole milk

1 cup shredded Monterey Jack cheese

There are plenty of recipes out there for "sneaking" vegetables into a plate of mac and cheese, but why hide them if the idea is to show children that vegetables can be delicious? This recipe does just that, using slow-roasted butternut squash in place of some of the cheese and milk.

Preheat the oven to 400°F.

Place the squash, cut-side up, on a baking sheet. Drizzle with the olive oil and season with salt and pepper. Bake until tender when pierced with a fork, 30 to 40 minutes. Remove the squash from the oven and allow to cool for 5 or 10 minutes. Leave the oven on and reduce the temperature to 350°F.

Meanwhile, bring a large pot of salted water to a boil over high heat. Add the pasta and cook according to the package instructions, or until just al dente. Drain the pasta and transfer to a large bowl.

When the squash is cool enough to handle, use a spoon to scoop the flesh into a food processor. Add the milk and puree until smooth. Add the squash puree to the pasta and fold together with a rubber spatula until combined.

Grease a 9-inch square or round baking dish. Spread the pasta mixture evenly in the dish and top with the cheese. Bake until the cheese is melted and the top is golden, 5 to 7 minutes. Let stand for 5 minutes before serving.

VEGETABLE
CHIPS

These are a little showoff-y for sure and maybe not super-practical to make every day. But if you find yourself with a surplus of, say, zucchini, and you've made enough zucchini bread, vegetable chips are fun, easy, and a delicious addition for a kid's birthday party.

Place a rack in the center of the oven and preheat to 250°F. Line two rimmed baking sheets with parchment paper.

With a mandoline or very sharp knife, very thinly slice each of the vegetables lengthwise. Arrange the vegetable slices in a single layer on the baking sheets and brush with the olive oil.

Bake for 30 minutes, then carefully flip the vegetables and return to the oven until the vegetables are crisp, 30 to 40 minutes longer.

Let the vegetables cool completely on the baking sheets, then transfer to an airtight container. They will last up to 2 weeks stored in a cool, dry place.

MAKES 3 ADULT SERVINGS
OR 6 KID SERVINGS

1 medium summer squash

1 zucchini

5 baby golden beets, scrubbed

1 medium parsnip, scrubbed

1 medium carrot, scrubbed

3 large kale leaves, rinsed well and torn into 1-inch pieces

3 tablespoons extra-virgin olive oil

STUFFED
SWEET POTATOES

This was an instant classic the first time I served it to my children. The salty-sweet combo of pineapple and ham makes a great filling for velvety sweet potatoes.

Preheat the oven to 400°F. Place the sweet potatoes directly on the oven rack and roast until they are soft when squeezed, 30 to 40 minutes. Set aside to cool.

In a large skillet, melt the butter over medium heat. Add the orange juice, lemon juice, soy sauce, and brown sugar. Once the orange juice mixture has started to bubble, add the ham and pineapple and cook, stirring occasionally, until the ham is crisp around the edges, 5 to 7 minutes.

With a sharp knife, make a lengthwise slit in the top of each sweet potato. Squeeze the potato open. Spoon some of the ham and pineapple into each potato. Serve 1 potato for each adult, or a half to each child, breaking it up with a fork if desired.

MAKES 4 ADULT SERVINGS
OR 8 KID SERVINGS

4 large sweet potatoes, scrubbed and pierced with a fork

1 tablespoon unsalted butter

1 cup orange juice

Juice of ½ lemon

2 tablespoons low-sodium soy sauce

1 tablespoon light brown sugar

½ pound cooked ham, cut into 1½-inch cubes

¾ cup fresh pineapple cubes (½ inch)

EGGPLANT PARMESAN

MAKES 4 TO 6 ADULT SERVINGS
OR 6 TO 8 KID SERVINGS

1 egg

¼ cup whole milk

2 cups panko breadcrumbs

4 tablespoons extra-virgin olive oil

1 medium eggplant, unpeeled, cut crosswise into ½-inch-thick slices

½ medium yellow onion, finely chopped

2 garlic cloves, finely chopped

1 can (28 ounces) whole peeled tomatoes

8 ounces fresh mozzarella cheese, cut into 1-inch cubes

4 ounces frozen spinach, thawed and drained, and most of the moisture squeezed out

2 tablespoons torn fresh basil leaves

This sped-up version of the classic eggplant Parmesan is super kid-friendly and tastes fantastic. Its soft texture allows it to be easily fork-mashed into kid servings. Feel free to add protein like bits of grilled chicken or sautéed ground lamb.

In a small bowl, beat the egg and milk together with a fork. Place the panko in a shallow dish.

In a large skillet, heat 2 tablespoons of the oil over medium-high heat. One at a time, dip the eggplant slices into the egg mixture, then dredge in the panko. Place in the hot skillet and cook until lightly golden on both sides, 3 to 4 minutes per side. Drain the slices on paper towels.

Wipe out the skillet and heat the remaining 2 tablespoons oil over medium heat. Add the onion and garlic and cook until the onion is translucent, 4 to 5 minutes. Add the tomatoes and their juices and use a wooden spoon to break the tomatoes into small chunks. Cook the tomatoes until the sauce has slightly thickened, 5 to 7 minutes.

Preheat the broiler.

Arrange the eggplant in a single layer in a 9 x 13-inch baking dish. Scatter the mozzarella and spinach over the eggplant, then spoon the tomato sauce evenly over all. Broil the eggplant until the cheese is golden and bubbling, 3 to 5 minutes. Serve garnished with the basil.

ONE-PAN
LASAGNA

As far as I'm concerned, this recipe is worth the price of the book—it's that good and that easy. You've probably spent hours making lasagna, carefully layering in the ingredients, only to find, when you serve it up, that it looks nothing like the perfect squares you envisioned. This version is all about flavor—who cares what it looks like? It requires just one pan and takes about 25 minutes to make, start to finish. Just try it. You'll never make a traditional lasagna again.

Preheat the oven to 400°F.

In a large ovenproof skillet, heat the oil over medium heat until shimmering. Add the beef and cook, breaking up with a wooden spatula, until the meat has browned, 5 to 7 minutes.

Meanwhile, combine the tomatoes, carrots, onion, and garlic in a food processor and chop until coarsely ground but not completely smooth.

When the meat is browned, pour off any accumulated fat. Add the tomato mixture, stock, ricotta, and spinach and combine thoroughly. Bury the lasagna noodles in the sauce, and sprinkle the mozzarella evenly over all.

Bake the lasagna uncovered until the cheese is melted and bubbling, 10 to 15 minutes. Remove the pan from the oven and let stand uncovered for 10 minutes. Serve warm.

MAKES 4 TO 6 ADULT SERVINGS
OR 8 KID SERVINGS

2 tablespoons extra-virgin olive oil

1 pound lean ground grass-fed beef

1 can (28 ounces) whole peeled tomatoes, preferably San Marzano

4 baby carrots, scrubbed

1 small yellow onion, cut into wedges

1 garlic clove, thinly sliced

1 cup organic chicken stock

½ cup part-skim ricotta cheese

3 ounces fresh spinach leaves, stems removed and coarsely chopped

4 lasagna noodles, broken into 1½-inch pieces

4 ounces fresh mozzarella, cubed

BARBECUE TURKEY MEATLOAF CUPCAKES WITH MASHED POTATO FROSTING

This was another one of my wife's brilliant ideas. Not only is this a really good recipe for a traditional meatloaf, but making it into little presents, like these cupcakes, makes my children feel they are getting something really special.

Preheat the oven to 400°F. Line the cups of a mini-muffin pan with paper liners.

In a large pot, combine the potatoes with enough water to cover. Season with salt and bring to a boil over medium-high heat. Cook the potatoes until tender when pierced with a fork, about 20 minutes. Drain the potatoes and return to the pot. Mash the potatoes until smooth.

In a skillet, heat the oil over medium heat. Add the onion and cook until translucent, 2 or 3 minutes. Set aside to cool.

In a large bowl, combine the cornbread and buttermilk. Stir and let stand for 5 minutes or until all the buttermilk has been absorbed. Add the sautéed onion, turkey, barbecue sauce, egg, and parsley and stir with clean hands until well blended.

Fill the muffin cups with the turkey mixture. Top each cupcake with a bacon slice. Bake until the bacon is crisp and the meat is cooked through, 20 to 25 minutes. Cool the meatloaf cupcakes for 5 minutes.

Use a pastry bag or butter knife to "frost" each cupcake with the potato mixture. Serve warm.

MAKES 12 MINI MEATLOAF CUPCAKES

2 medium russet (baking) potatoes, peeled and cut into 1-inch chunks

Pinch of salt

2 tablespoons extra-virgin olive oil

⅓ small white onion, finely chopped

¾ cup coarsely crumbled cornbread

2 tablespoons buttermilk

1 pound ground turkey

¼ cup barbecue sauce

1 large egg

2 tablespoons chopped fresh parsley

2 slices thick-cut bacon, cut crosswise into 1-inch strips

TURKEY MEATBALL STROGANOFF

MAKES 4 TO 6 ADULT SERVINGS
OR 8 KID SERVINGS

1 slice multigrain bread

1½ pounds ground turkey

2 tablespoons whole milk

½ medium yellow onion, minced

½ teaspoon caraway seeds, crushed

Pinch of salt

2 tablespoons extra-virgin olive oil

1 garlic clove, chopped

6 ounces white mushrooms, thinly sliced

1 sprig thyme

1 tablespoon unbleached all-purpose flour

1½ cups chicken stock

2 tablespoons sour cream

2 teaspoons Dijon mustard

8 ounces cooked egg noodles

2 tablespoons chopped fresh parsley

Ground turkey is the go-to protein when we are cooking for our children at home. Even ground turkey can taste as delicious as a roasted Thanksgiving bird if you give it a good browning to caramelize the meat juices. Remember: Color equals flavor. This whole meal comes together with a classic Stroganoff sauce that is so good I bet it makes it into your weekly rotation.

Remove the crust from the bread slice and tear the bread into small pieces. In a large bowl, mix the turkey together with the bread, milk, onion, caraway seeds, and salt until combined. With wet hands, shape the turkey mixture into about eighteen 1½-inch meatballs.

In a large skillet, heat the oil over medium heat until shimmering. Add the meatballs and cook, turning often, until browned, 5 to 7 minutes. Transfer the meatballs to a plate.

Add the garlic to the same skillet and cook over medium heat for a minute or two. Add the mushrooms and thyme and continue to cook, turning often, until the mushrooms are golden. Sprinkle the flour over the mushrooms and stir to coat. Stir in the chicken stock and cook, stirring often, until the sauce has thickened, 5 to 7 minutes.

Whisk in the sour cream and mustard until smooth, then return the meatballs to the pan. Turn to coat with the sauce.

Spoon the meatballs and sauce over the noodles and serve garnished with the parsley.

HALIBUT FISH STICKS WITH GREEN BEANS AND POTATOES

MAKES 4 ADULT SERVINGS
OR 6 KID SERVINGS

½ cup plus 2 tablespoons buttermilk

1 pound skinless halibut fillet, cut into
1-inch-wide fingers

1 cup panko breadcrumbs

2 teaspoons fresh thyme leaves

Salt and freshly ground pepper

½ pound assorted baby potatoes,
scrubbed and quartered

½ pound green beans

2 tablespoons extra-virgin olive oil

½ cup mayonnaise

½ cup sour cream

2 tablespoons sweet pickle relish

1 tablespoon capers, finely chopped

2 tablespoons chopped fresh parsley

The last time I checked, some of the fish sticks from the grocery store freezer section were not exactly what I would call 100 percent fish. Many contain some kind of filler or stabilizer that makes them, literally, the chicken nuggets of the sea. Fresh, wild Alaskan halibut is a perfect way to introduce your children to fish: It's sustainable and plentiful and has a delicious, mild flavor. This is not just for kids, by the way; it could become your go-to fish recipe for an adult dinner party, as well.

Preheat the oven to 400°F. Line a rimmed baking sheet with parchment paper.

Pour ½ cup of the buttermilk into a large bowl. Add the halibut pieces and turn to coat. In another bowl, stir together the panko, thyme, and salt and pepper to taste. Dredge each fish finger in the breadcrumbs to coat completely and arrange at one end of the baking sheet.

Combine the potatoes and green beans in a bowl and drizzle with the oil. Toss to coat thoroughly, then arrange the vegetables at the other end of the baking sheet. Bake the fish and vegetables, turning once, until the fish fingers are golden, about 12 minutes.

Stir together the mayonnaise, sour cream, relish, capers, and parsley until well blended. Thin with the remaining 2 tablespoons buttermilk and season with salt and pepper. Serve with the fish and veggies.

BAKED PUMPKIN
AND PEACHES

You'd never find this flavor combination in nature, because pumpkin and peaches are a complete 180 from one another in terms of growing seasons. To keep things seasonal, you can use frozen peaches during pumpkin season and canned pumpkin puree during peach season. Either way you'll have a very healthy dessert for children and adults alike that tastes amazing. For a cool presentation, use a second pumpkin that you roast along with the wedges as a baking dish.

Preheat the oven to 350°F. Line a rimmed baking sheet with parchment paper.

Cut the pumpkin into 8 to 10 wedges and remove the seeds. Set aside ½ cup of the peach slices for the topping, and arrange the remaining peach slices and the pumpkin wedges on the baking sheet until the pumpkin is tender when pierced with a fork, 25 to 30 minutes. Leave the oven on.

Peel the pumpkin wedges and place the flesh in a food processor. Add the baked peach slices, maple syrup, nutmeg, and salt and puree until smooth.

In a bowl, crush the graham crackers together with the brown sugar and butter using a large spoon.

Spoon the puree into a baking dish. Top with the graham cracker mixture and remaining peach slices and bake until the butter has melted and the top is golden, 10 to 15 minutes. Serve hot.

MAKES 4 TO 6 ADULT SERVINGS
OR 6 TO 8 KID SERVINGS

1 small pumpkin or kabocha squash
(1 to 1 ½ pounds)

1 bag (16 ounces) frozen peach slices

3 tablespoons maple syrup

¼ teaspoon freshly grated nutmeg

Pinch of salt

5 whole graham crackers, crushed

2 tablespoons dark brown sugar

2 tablespoons cold unsalted butter

STRAWBERRY-STUFFED MUFFINS

MAKES 24 MINI MUFFINS

2 cups unbleached all-purpose flour

1 cup granulated sugar

1 tablespoon baking powder

½ teaspoon salt

3 eggs, lightly beaten

1 cup whole milk

2 tablespoons unsalted butter, melted

½ teaspoon pure vanilla extract

12 medium strawberries, halved

½ cup confectioners' sugar

2 teaspoons fresh lemon juice

These look especially cute made as mini muffins, but you can also make them in standard muffins tins. If you make the larger muffins, increase the baking time to 12 to 15 minutes and place 2 strawberry halves on each unbaked muffin.

Preheat the oven to 400°F. Line a 24-cup mini-muffin tin with paper liners.

In a large bowl, whisk together the flour, granulated sugar, baking powder, and salt. In a large measuring cup, whisk together the eggs, milk, butter, and vanilla.

Add the milk mixture to the flour mixture and stir just until well blended. Scoop the batter into the prepared muffin cups, filling each two-thirds full. Top each with a strawberry half.

Bake the muffins until the tops are golden and a toothpick inserted in the center comes out clean, 10 to 12 minutes. Cool the muffins in the pan for 10 minutes before glazing.

In a small bowl, mix the confectioners' sugar with the lemon juice and stir until smooth. Drizzle the muffins with the glaze, and allow to cool completely.

APPLE GINGER GRANITA

3 cups unfiltered apple juice

3 tablespoons honey

1 teaspoon grated peeled fresh ginger

When your children are under the weather—which some-times feels like every other day at my house—it's nice to have something soothing for a sore throat that's not "med-icine." Ginger is an amazing home remedy that has been used to treat stomach upset, diarrhea, and nausea for more than 2,000 years. The root contains pungent phenol com-pounds that also reduce inflammation, which makes it per-fect for a sore throat. So when my little ones really need a pick-me-up, this delicious granita does the trick.

In a large saucepan, combine the apple juice, honey, and ginger. Add 1 cup water and bring to a boil over medium heat. Remove the pan from the heat and set aside to cool for 20 minutes.

When the mixture has cooled, pour it into a 9 x 13-inch glass baking dish. Cover the dish tightly with plastic wrap and place in the freezer for at least 2 hours, or until frozen solid.

Use a fork to scrape the granita into serving cups.

ROASTED RED PEARS
WITH RICOTTA

Slow-roasted, natural fruit flavors are one of the hallmarks of Sprout baby food. Slow-cooking the fruit naturally gives it a sweeter flavor and softer texture that babies love. You can also pulse the fruit and ricotta together in the food processor for a smooth texture similar to pudding.

Preheat the oven to 400°F. Line a rimmed baking sheet with parchment paper.

Use a melon baller to scoop out the core and seeds from each pear half, then arrange the pears, cut-side up, on the baking sheet. Top with the cinnamon sticks and drizzle the pear halves with 1 tablespoon of the maple syrup.

Roast the pears for 30 to 40 minutes, or until they have released their juices and browned slightly but are still holding their shape. Discard the cinnamon sticks and let the pears cool for 5 minutes or so.

In a small bowl, stir together the ricotta cheese and cinnamon.

Serve the pears warm with a dollop of the spiced ricotta. Drizzle with the remaining tablespoon of maple syrup and top with crumbled cookies if you like.

MAKES 4 SERVINGS

2 red Anjou pears, halved

2 whole cinnamon sticks, broken into pieces

2 tablespoons pure maple syrup

½ cup whole-milk ricotta cheese

⅛ teaspoon ground cinnamon, plus more for sprinkling

2 or 3 oatmeal raisin cookies (optional)

ACKNOWLEDGMENTS

Doing this book was a true family project. Having people in our home shooting and cooking for a few weeks at a time is a fairly intimate experience with a house full of kids, dogs, and a new puppy. Our friends John Lee and Kevin Crafts arrived every morning with fresh coffee, beautiful ingredients, and a whole bunch of patience and love. Having them in our house day in, day out was like having friends over for summer camp.

John Lee, you are an artist. Having you in our lives the past few years has been so special. You are capturing our children's lives as they grow up, and we will always be thankful for these beautiful images.

Kevin Crafts, you get kids. You also do perfect recipes right alongside me with the laptop on the kitchen counter, all while making the plate look perfect for each shot.

My wife, Tolan—thank you for our beautiful children and for a house full of mix-and-match antiques, platters, plates, and BPA-free sippy cups. Once again, we were able to shoot an entire book without buying props or going any farther than our garage. And Christina Flach—thanks for your great work on hair and makeup.

A huge shout-out to our special ladies, Hilda and Alana. They take care of our family and our home—and never get upset with me when I trash the kitchen. We couldn't do it without them.

Pam Krauss, your cup runneth over with patience, guidance, and impeccable taste. Thank you for making my books what they are. To the entire team at Rodale and especially Kara Plikaitis, Zachary Greenwald, Yelena Nesbit, and Olivia Baniuszewicz.

And a special thank-you to my partners and team members at Sprout.

INDEX

Boldfaced page references indicate photographs.